transforming lives together

What people are saying about …

GROWING KIDS WITH CHARACTER

"Hettie Brittz invites you to an enriching and educational counseling session that answers every possible question regarding your child's temperament and associating traits. Hettie addresses the reader in such a personal and loving way that parents, as well as professionals, will feel equipped to meet the challenges of parenthood and to better understand their children, or clients or patients. This book not only changed the way I parent my own children but also enhanced my therapy with my patients, both children and parents."

Jo-Marie vdM-Bothma, PhD (Psych)

"This phenomenal book combines authenticity from an author who lives out the wisdom she offers, practical help that takes into account the uniqueness of your family, and a healthy dose of grace, because none of us have it all perfectly worked out and yet our heavenly Father loves us unconditionally."

Graeme Schnell, CEO of Focus
on the Family Africa

"For the last three decades I have worked closely with kids of various ages in various countries—as a teacher, an aunt, a youth group leader, and in a leadership role with Compassion International. I wish I had had access to Hettie's insights through *Growing Kids with*

Character years ago! It would have been a helpful lens into the souls of the kids who crossed my path. Whether you're a parent or not, if you regularly work with children, this book is a must-read."

Adéle Booysen, DMin, chief adventure
guide at BlueThread.Life

"Relationships! Life hinges on relationship with God and man. I have seen families being transformed when parents understand the need-behaviors of their children, and learn to adapt and respond to these needs. Hettie Brittz has developed a psychometric tool that succinctly aligns child behaviors to tree images, to help parents and children understand the dynamics of intra- and interpersonal relationships for life."

Dr. Khoo Oon Theam, international
coach in psychometric instrumentation,
leadership, and organization behavior

"While I can safely claim that the content of this book rescued me from a number of parenting blunders, it also enriched my work with parents and children. Hettie Brittz offers creative and spot-on explanations for challenging parent-child interactions, and her discipline advice lends itself to a balanced approach to childhood development. Hettie manages to make the journey both light and deep—pointing you to the mileposts of good communication and effective behavior management, while keeping your sanity about you."

Professor Rika Swanzen, PhD, program leader
of child and youth care at Monash South Africa

"At age twenty-eight, I married a widower and father of six children. Despite my experience as a teacher, I felt overwhelmed, trying to understand seven different personalities all at once. I leaned heavily on the information about the different character tree types in *Growing Kids with Character*. I absolutely love how the descriptions allow me to visualize and remember what each character type embodies as we navigate this journey we are on. I strongly encourage anyone, especially parents in blended families, to read what Hettie has written. This knowledge empowers and brings light where we cannot see the way."

Chani Zimmerman, instant mother of six

growing
kids with
character

HETTIE BRITTZ

growing kids with character

NURTURING YOUR CHILD'S POTENTIAL, PURPOSE, AND PASSION

DAVID C COOK

transforming lives together

GROWING KIDS WITH CHARACTER
Published by David C Cook
4050 Lee Vance Drive
Colorado Springs, CO 80918 U.S.A.

David C Cook U.K., Kingsway Communications
Eastbourne, East Sussex BN23 6NT, England

The graphic circle C logo is a registered trademark of David C Cook.

The website addresses recommended throughout this book are offered as a
resource to you. These websites are not intended in any way to be or imply an
endorsement on the part of David C Cook, nor do we vouch for their content.

Details in some stories have been changed to protect the identities of the persons involved.

LCCN 2017952719
ISBN 978-1-4347-1253-0
eISBN 978-0-8307-7275-9

© 2018 Hettie Brittz

The Team: Alice Crider, Erin Healy, Nick Lee, Jack Campbell, Susan Murdock
Cover Design: Amy Konyndyk

Printed in the United States of America
First Edition 2018

1 2 3 4 5 6 7 8 9 10

121917

CONTENTS

ACKNOWLEDGMENTS

Thank You, Lord Jesus, for putting me in parenting ministry despite my parenting mistakes (past, present, and future). It is Your grace that I treasure most! Please extend the same to each home through these pages.

What I know about parenting is perhaps like a building. I would like to thank my parents, Petru and Ida Gräbe, for the foundation, walls, and roof. The rest is just furnishings—you gave me a worthy example, biblical truth, and your brand of common sense.

My children—Idalise, Pero, and Simoné—thank you for the windows of enlightenment (usually installed in hindsight and replaced many times over, of course!) through which I now look at other kids and their parents with a lot less arrogance. And thank you for not breaking, locking, or hiding my laptop, even though it had been your enemy for so many months.

Louis, you are so much more than just my husband. Thank you for believing in my ability to climb this mountain. Thank you for the late-night coffee next to my computer and for taking the kids on outings when I had to put in long hours of work. You see my shortcomings as a parent on a daily basis. Thank you for completing me rather than complaining about me at such times!

A big thank-you to all the parents who share their struggles and joys with me. I learn a lot from you and your children. Thank you for the encouragement to write this book. Thank you for your numerous questions, which helped me to bring theory and practice closer together.

Thank you to Carpe Diem Media, the first publisher of this book in Afrikaans, my mother tongue. You turned me into a writer. Thank you, Alice, Matt, Cris, and the team at David C Cook, who turned me into an international author.

I also have to acknowledge all the authors and speakers who have inspired me with their passion for parenting. I have listed your life-changing books in the notes section and in the featured quotes throughout these pages. Even when I don't quote you page and verse, you speak in my head, from the same Source of wisdom I try to tap into. I can think of no greater honor than to stand next to you and equip parents with creative solutions to grow kids with character, perfect for their purpose in God.

INTRODUCTION

Oh, the optimism!

My children and I were very excited about our first attempt at a vegetable garden. How hard could it be? To my husband's dismay, we dug out almost the entire lawn behind the swimming pool. We planted eight different vegetables and believed that everything would flourish. How self-sufficient we would be! In my mind I could already see myself smugly passing the expensive grocery store around the corner.

We started planting at exactly the right time of year. Fertilizer, water, and sunshine were all aplenty. Each morning we would tiptoe over the dewy lawn to check on our progress. The carrots and onions didn't surface right away, but most of the other seeds sprouted happily, and the small plants were soon several centimeters high—as green as grass and promising! I took photos of every phase.

Oh, the unexpected!

Shortly after this, nasty cutworms and spiders started attacking. Almost everything stopped growing, and upon closer inspection we discovered that more worms than roots were attached to the spinach seedlings. Despite the row of caper bushes that were supposed to repel them, snails came like pilgrims from faraway lands, leaving shiny trails. By the time I was equipped with sprays, pellets, and powders, only a failed harvest remained. Our nightly snail hunt was a huge adventure for my son, with flashlight and trap in hand, but alas, it was just not effective enough to stem the tide of the slimy prowlers.

When I started asking around (with a sense of shame) whether everyone struggled as much as I did, I got the impression that other vegetable growers did many things differently. Apparently we planted the wrong kind of beans and supported them incorrectly. Apparently the spacing instructions on the back of the seed packets were important! Apparently those onions really had to sprout in seed trays first. Had I done anything right?

Well, there were the record-breaking squashes. I took lots of photographs of the first whoppers as they lay heavily on the kitchen scale, and I bragged shamelessly. I would have Facebooked, Instagrammed, pinned, and tweeted them, but this was before the days of social media. These marrows were the result of perfectly aligned conditions in the soils and the weather—not an accurate reflection of my gardening talents!

Oh, the misfortune!

A few weeks later, an unexpected hailstorm flattened the only surviving white pumpkins, which had been showing signs of creeping all the way around the swimming pool (one is allowed to exaggerate about one's vegetable garden). My children's homemade "scared-to-death-crow" lost its shiny Christmas decorations and fluttering ribbons to the hailstorm, and winged pests had no respect for the old mop with the crocodile T-shirt. They finished off what the storm had left.

What can I say? The local grocery store kept us as clients!

Oh, the disillusionment!

The whole business of growing plants is difficult, but growing children is even more difficult. Everything starts out so well, and the baby pictures show so much promise. Before the birth, we read everything we can find about childcare on both spiritual and emotional levels. We establish rules for our household.

The children learn to walk, to talk, and even to pray at the right time. The years pass so quickly, and then, unexpectedly, all kinds of pests and plagues strike. They threaten the fruit of years of parenting. Sometimes we fear permanent damage, as with our hailstorm. Instead of a promising harvest, we reap misunderstanding and rebellion.

Some parents give up when this happens, as I did with the vegetable garden. They resign themselves to the defeat that "it is natural" for kids to go off the rails. Is it? Or is it all our fault?

We'd all love to be natural moms and dads with kids who have great character. Instead, most of us feel unnatural at the task, as I did at gardening, and our kids are the ones who are natural—natural rebels, natural criers, natural sleepers, natural manipulators, natural charmers, or natural escape artists. What are we to do with these natural tendencies—good and bad?

Oh, the starting over!

Doomsayers tell us that we basically can do nothing for our children's character after their sixth birthday—the window of opportunity has closed. They tell us our kids are shaped forever and will not learn anything new. But this rules out God and all His wonderful grace and power. This underestimates the wonder of second chances. This loses sight of what can happen when a parent gets back into the garden with renewed resolve to shake things up. Of course there is a chance for a new beginning.

Typical kids can become kids of great character when we point them to God's blueprint for their individual potential, purpose, and passion.

Sometimes our children are anxiously awaiting any sign that we want to improve so that they can lay down their weapons. We may feel like we are opposing forces, but if we can figure out how that happened, we can get back on the same side and miracles can happen in a short amount of time. Wouldn't it be wonderful if, by the grace of God, we could have a harvest that needs no exaggeration? What if we could grow children we can be openly proud of and thankful for—like those squashes of mine? Maybe even I, who can't keep a fern alive, could shape tender saplings to grow tall and straight. Maybe you could grow a tree that is heavy with fruit! Maybe all our kids can grow into God's perfect plan for them. I believe it.

Oh, the discovery!

Can we expect to cultivate healthy young trees without understanding how they function? Should we all sit around the tea table like a bunch of old ladies and sigh and say, "Oh, if only the children came with an instruction manual"? I believe they did! And I am referring not only to the Bible. Into every child's beautifully unique nature, the answers to a million questions are written. Which type of child should be left to cry alone, and which should be cuddled into a smile after tears? How do I motivate the child who never "feels like it"? How should a father get his teenager's attention when she pretends that he is invisible?

When the questions and their answers are this diverse, and our children find such original ways to mess up, we need more than just Five Steps or Seven Keys to be perfect parents. I have read many "foolproof" parenting books that promise, "Just do as we say, and your family will look like the photo on the back cover of this book in no time." Father, mother, and children are sitting happily in a little boat on crystal-clear water with drooping willows framing the picture idyllically in green. We want to be like them, so we do exactly as the book tells us to do, but it doesn't work for us. Are we to blame? Are our children perhaps to blame? Or are the writers of those books to blame? No, no, and no. What's to blame is the naive assumption that one plan could work for everyone.

This book will help you know which plan is right for you and your child. While not perfect, your child is going to be a natural at stepping into the plan that God gave when He breathed life into him or her. Your journey will be unique. It is guaranteed to be a gardening adventure! May the Lord be present in your "nursery" in full force. May your saplings each reflect the multiple wonders of the Lord and glorify Him through their unique character!

Hettie Brittz

CHAPTER 1

ON YOUR MARKS, GET SET, GROW!

In this chapter:

- How can we better prepare ourselves for parenting?
- We need shaping just as much as our children need it.
- Our past ought to make way for a new vision.
- We can emulate God as the Great Gardener.

Let's be honest. I'll go first and admit that I underestimated the importance of emotional readiness for parenting. I was prepared in every other respect. And being prepared for parenthood turned out to be more than having a stroller and a car seat or savings for your unborn child's education. The digital camera's batteries may be recharged and a large memory chip may be inserted for the 1,001 pictures of the birth and newborn days, but even then a parent's heart might not be ready to give what is most needed.

Readiness starts with basic maturity—the mind-set of no longer living only for yourself and your own needs but for someone else as well. Readiness for parenting also means that you start thinking about what you will invest in your children. It's about an eternal legacy, because they will probably outlive you!

> *To make a baby is one of the actions for which you need the least skills. It takes almost no experience, talent or expertise. Even people who can't throw a Frisbee, switch on the video machine or keep a job can make a baby.*
>
> Erma Bombeck, *Motherhood, the Second Oldest Profession*

Readiness also reflects a softened heart that is ready to learn about love and to receive help in the process. It is a mind-set that acknowledges, "I am not the whole story when it comes to parenting. God, other parents, life, friends, and influences will parent with me. I will deserve neither all the blame nor all the glory. I will be stretched in the process."

How can we better prepare ourselves for parenting? Reading books and attending a clinic or parenting talks will help, but we also need to sort out some deeper things in ourselves. Keep these three principles in mind:

1. We need shaping just as much as our children need it.
2. Our past ought to make way for a new plan.
3. We can emulate God as the Great Gardener.

WE NEED SHAPING JUST AS MUCH AS OUR CHILDREN NEED IT

Our first question as parents is usually: What can I do with this child? Actually, the question should be: What could I become for this child?

The answer is straightforward: I can invite the Great Gardener (God) to prune me even as I am pruning my saplings, and to shape me while I am shaping my young ones so we might all bear fruit (John 15:2).

Mistakes don't disqualify us from being parents, provided that we understand one thing: a parent living surrendered to Jesus is a better example of a Christ follower than a parent who tries to fake perfection, just as a rusty sign pointing in the right direction is better than a shiny new sign pointing in the wrong direction. So we may not be perfect, but we can always be forgiven and try again.

This book will suggest ways in which we parents can shape our discipline, our dialect, our dedication, our direction, and our discipling of our kids, with the goal of pruning them according to God's design for their individual personality types.

OUR PAST OUGHT TO MAKE WAY FOR A NEW PLAN

Those of us who want to be good parents may need to leave these two things behind:

1. The example set by our parents
2. Our own unpleasant parenting experiences

Why would we leave behind our parents' example?

A marriage is the start of a new family, and many young couples have trouble letting go of their families of origin in a healthy way. When it comes to disciplining children, however, a family cannot afford to have more than two parents, each with his or her own opinion, in one house. Many homes already have two parents who can't agree. Add additional voices whispering in the parents' ears, telling them how their mother or father would have acted in the situation, and you'll have as many as six opinions and constant conflict under one roof.

Those of us who have good childhood memories and who had a secure relationship with our parents are especially at risk of doing exactly what they did and what would please them, without thinking for ourselves. I am calling it a risk because the demands on parents have changed a lot during the past twenty years, and even if you learned good things from your parents, you can't discipline in the same way they did. And even if you could, it would not prepare your child for today's world. To do what they did may even be against the law now!

There is another, more important, reason to avoid using a "copy and paste" approach to parenting: you are not like your child any more than your parents were exactly like you when you were a kid. Your purpose and journey differ greatly from the plans God has for your kids.

Good parenting is proactive rather than reactive. This means having your own plan based on the purposes God reveals for your kids and not just blindly following someone else's example of what (or what not) to do. Are you spanking because you were spanked and "turned out fine"? Are you not spanking because your parents spanked you in anger? Are you using time-out because "all the other people at church believe in it"? Are you encouraging your child down a certain career path because your parents wouldn't allow you to follow it?

If you cannot give a good reason for your parenting style or method, you may not be able to hold your own against manipulative toddlers, nagging family members and friends, or this year's ten top tips for toddler training. You could become a chameleon parent experimenting on your children instead of an intentional gardener who prepares the soil, fertilizes the saplings intelligently, and lives to see the fruit mature as your kids enter into God's purpose for them.

If your childhood memories are riddled with painful moments, you may want to rewrite those hurts through the way you parent your children. This potentially dangerous strategy is reactive and often based on a one-sided perspective of what happened many years ago. For your children's sake, it's more important to discern God's calling on your child's life and cooperate with Him to make it a reality.

Allow me to share a story.

I was thirty-two and already the mom of two kids. Any emotional outburst on their part plunged me into panic because I had made a private vow that I would never let them cry a desperate cry without responding with everything I had. Yet, I also knew that children could use those gut-wrenching cries to manipulate. My inner conflict was unbearable: Do I give in, or do I ignore the cries of a little one who wants me back in the room after bedtime? Do I race back in, or do I walk away from the preschool classroom while my daughter is screaming my name?

My vow came from a memory of when I was only three years old. This is how I remember that day: My mom dropped me off for a playdate at our German friends' house. Mom was in a hurry, but I was clingy. Exasperated, she turned to her friend and said, "Heidi, just take her from me, please!" The woman pulled me off my mom, and my mom left. In my three-year-old mind, the expression on my mom's face was anger. I fell to the ground for a tantrum of note. The older children made a circle around me and imitated my sobs. They teased me in German. I felt utterly abandoned.

Twenty-nine years later, a wise mentor sat me down and helped me deal with this memory. She had the wisdom to realize that what I remembered probably was only part of the story, and she knew that my being a good mom would depend on moving beyond this hurt. If I couldn't, my aim as a mom would remain very small; it would simply be to never let the same thing happen to my children. But God wanted me to do something much bigger: to raise kids who knew their purpose!

My mentor prayed me through that memory. As I recalled the moment, I saw Jesus with us on the sidewalk, His arm around my mom's shoulders and compassion for her all over His face. I saw her face more clearly now, and her expression wasn't anger or frustration; it was sadness mixed with apprehension. She didn't know which way to go.

I became upset and told my mentor I didn't understand why Jesus felt sorry for my mom or why my mom seemed so lost. Wasn't I lost and hurting too? Yet, all my anger toward my mom melted away as I saw the picture in a whole new light. I felt sorry for her. I suddenly questioned all the other memories that "proved" she didn't care for my feelings. I recalled situations where I had assumed she had acted out of annoyance, but now I could imagine other explanations. I gave in to the overwhelming urge to drive to her house to find out what had really happened that day.

I started our conversation with this confession: "Mom, God showed me today that even though I thought you were sometimes deliberately hurtful, you never did anything to purposely hurt me."

My mom wept as she also recounted the many times she had failed to show me how much she cared. She made me tea when it was coffee I wanted. She bought me clothes in styles and colors I didn't like. "I feel as if there has always been something standing right between us, twisting every word and action," she concluded. She was absolutely right!

This was her side of the story: She and Heidi had met during prebirth checkups at the hospital. They both expected twins, and my mom, being fluent in German, made a connection that turned into a friendship. They gave birth on the same day and roomed in the same ward. My twin brother and I were born healthy. Heidi's baby boy died, and her little girl was born with severe cerebral palsy. The special bond and friendship continued, and Heidi kept requesting that I have playdates with her daughter. My compassionate mom waited until she felt I was ready. She prepared me for the visit and chose a suitable day, when she would be passing through their neighborhood for another commitment on her way to a show at the State Theatre. She would drop me off before the show and pick me up afterward.

Upon arrival at Heidi's house, I was no longer up for the visit, but my mom had all the theater tickets for herself and some friends. In these days before mobile phones, she had no way to make an alternative arrangement. She was caught among three impossibly hard decisions: Should she take me home and let down all her friends waiting at the theater? Should she take a three-year-old to the theater without a ticket while also disappointing Heidi, who had anticipated the visit for a long time? Or should she stick to the plan and pray I would get over the bout of separation anxiety and have a fun time? She chose the last option, but not without her heart breaking.

This explained the arm Jesus placed around her shoulder. I saw His gesture as saying, "Oh, sweet mom. You are doing the best you can here. You are making a painful choice for the sake of others and—very unfairly—there is going to be a price to pay. Your daughter will misunderstand and hold this against you for many years. She will believe the lie that you don't feel her pain. She'll put up a wall of defense, and many of your attempts to love her will fail to scale that wall. But I will bring a day when she will see the truth. And even this is part of her shaping for a special purpose."

Many things changed in an instant that day when Mom and I finally talked about the memory. My mom's true heart became visible. Deep down I had always known how thoughtful and compassionate she was, though I could never give her credit. Instead of feeling she owed me an apology, I felt great remorse at how hard I had been on her for decades. Instead of wanting to do everything different from her, I came to see her as my best friend and role model. Even today I try to be more like her. I have my own parenting convictions now; however, they are no longer a response to pain—they are a proactive plan.

As for my purpose, God always knew He would put me in parenting ministry someday. My name means "star of hope," and I needed a revelation of God's hope for every broken relationship. Through this painful experience, I learned that even decades of misunderstanding can turn into deep friendship and respect. I don't believe in irreconcilable differences, incompatible personalities, or doomed families. I have evidence and experience to the contrary, thanks to the day my mom and I thought she had messed it all up.

Will my children misunderstand some of my actions? Absolutely. Will they make inner vows that start with, "I will never do what she did when …"? Probably. When their first babies are born, I will tell them this story and urge them to begin their parenting years with truth and forgiveness of past hurts. To start new. To start untriggered. To believe in God's purpose even in parenting pain.

> *Friends, don't get me wrong: By no means do I count myself an expert in all of this, but I've got my eye on the goal, where God is beckoning us onward—to Jesus. I'm off and running, and I'm not turning back.*
>
> Philippians 3:13–14

How can we start over if our own parenting mistakes haunt us?

Almost all parents who feel that they have failed harbor such feelings because of one or more incidents of conflict with their children. This means that someone is guilty, someone is angry, someone is sorry, someone is sad, or someone is lonely. All these emotions make the problems seem bigger than they really are. Therefore, we would be wise to pray for perspective before we can tackle the problem.

A mistake is not necessarily an indication of poor parenting. We ought to rectify what we can, but we also need to know that we will make many mistakes over the course of our children's lives. This is allowed in parenting! It's helpful and healthy to identify the events that have led to our feelings of failure and try to solve them as best we can. Unfortunately, if we sweep these things under the carpet, eventually we have to get them back out. The feelings of sadness, guilt, or bitterness will not go away until we deal with them. They are smoke signals that lead us to the smoldering fire of unresolved issues.

Prayerfully tackle one issue at a time. If your children are adults, try being frank: "It still bothers me that I [name what you think you did wrong]. This is how I think it damaged our relationship … Is that what you feel too?"[1] Once you both have given your side of the incident, be the adult in the room. Don't defend your words or actions. Ask for forgiveness. Repeat this process as often as needed until all the lies and vows and mantras float belly up in the sea of God's good plans for both of you.

Sometimes the only forgiveness that is needed is the forgiveness of ourselves—something we can learn to do in prayer. Forgiving yourself is simply giving yourself less credit while giving God more. "I have not destroyed my kids, because God's love and purpose for them are greater than my failures. My sin is not so exceptional that the suffering and death of Jesus could atone for everyone but me. I can be forgiven, and all the damage I have done can be redeemed, thanks to God's grace!" After repenting of our parenting failures, we should make an effort to discipline our thoughts, keeping them from dwelling on these past hurts.

Perhaps your children's bad behavior haunts you more than your own. Like your own mistakes, a child's serious blunder is not necessarily a sign of bad parenting. Sometimes we can do everything right and still have to look on as our children make poor choices. That is the reality of freedom of choice. Our children can say yes or no to our parenting advice.

Imagine the difference in your relationship if you could forget their worst fiasco and give them a new start each day. Forgiving them is the same process as forgiving yourself. Give your child less credit and God more. Your child has not out-sinned every other sinner. Jesus has canceled those mistakes effectively. Your child is not beyond salvation, because God is not intimidated by human devastation. He is a Master Rebuilder!

Will you allow yourself and your children to start over? The Lord is ready to help you through His Spirit.

WE CAN EMULATE GOD AS THE GREAT GARDENER

We emulate God in three aspects of parenting—presence, priorities, and purpose.

Our role as parents will change significantly over the years, but we never leave the stage. Diaper duty makes way for carpool turns and later for high school party supervision. Initially, we enjoy the spotlight and play a major part in our children's lives, but later on we play less central roles, and eventually we may even become part of the props. Nevertheless, we remain written into our children's life scripts forever. We emulate God's parenting *presence.*

The Bible shows us a hands-on God. He literally gets His hands dirty when He makes His first son and puts His own breath in him (Genesis 2:7). He provides Eden and Eve—a delightful environment and means to fulfill every need. He forges an intimate relationship by being close and speaking to His children. He makes rules, like any good parent, and He announces and enforces consequences for sin (Genesis 3). Throughout it all, He gives great grace. He equips His children to live as wonderful beings and to make Him known in the world.

There is no other model for parents to follow.

We also need to emulate God's parenting *priorities*. He is all about family! He makes us sons and daughters and binds every believer together into one household (2 Corinthians 6:18; Galatians 4:5; Ephesians 2:19). He regards the way we treat our family as our most important testimony and our key credibility check as leaders (1 Timothy 3:4; 5:8).

Yet many ambitions and desires war against the health of our families, don't they? During a season when I was definitely more concerned with my career than my kids (God help me, I often still am!), Psalm 127 caught my eye. It holds a stern caution that we may be wasting our time by rising early and staying up late toiling for what is temporary (food, clothes, promotion, and a roof over our head), because the Lord grants sleep to those He loves. Sleep? Does He really mean that a sign of His approval is not wealth or perfect kids, but instead rest? Not a grand house or medals and trophies, but instead peaceful sleep? Not all the stuff that symbolize success, but instead those sweet faces we wake up to in the morning (and often several times at night)? This psalm says that it is not God driving us to all this striving. Verses 3 through 5 remind us that children are "God's best gift," a reward from Him, and our "generous legacy."

Clearly the psalmist understood something of this apparent juggling act between building a life and raising kids. He unlocks the truth for us: raising children *is* building a life. Don't confuse it with the accumulation of wealth or climbing corporate and social ladders.

There is another noteworthy aspect to God's parenting: He doesn't treat all of His children the same. He makes each of them unique with unique gifts (1 Corinthians 12:4–6, 29–30). This is His parenting *purpose.* He places a calling on their lives and guides each into his or her own journey (1 Corinthians 7:17). Each of God's children even receives tailor-made grace (Ephesians 4:7) and individualized rewards (1 Corinthians 3:8; Revelation 22:12). Emulating our Gardener in this way means giving up on the idea of raising superkids according to *our* vision for their lives, and instead parenting our unique children according to their God-given design. We are called to the challenge and adventure of identifying that design in each of our children and prayerfully pruning it into a God-glorifying thing of beauty!

LET'S GET PRACTICAL

Prayerfully ask yourself these questions to discern the current effectiveness of your parenting approach. Take the answers to God for His grace and guidance as you step into His calling as the parent your children need.

Am I willing to be shaped as much as I shape my kids?

- Am I willingly connected to the True Vine and open to the pruning of the Great Gardener? How has He used parenting to shape me?
- Am I going to allow parenting to transform my heart, or am I going to keep my heart to myself and embark on parenting in such a way that my heart is locked up and guarded?
- What am I trying to change in my child even though I have not yet changed in that area?

Am I willing to exchange the past for a new vision?

- What is my worst memory of being parented? Am I believing a lie about my parents' intentions? Am I ready to forgive and move on?
- What are the three most important things I want to give my children? Why are these things so important to me?
- What is my biggest parenting failure? Who should still forgive me—God, my children, my spouse, or myself? What can I do about it today?
- What hope can I derive from Isaiah 49:24–25 and 58:9–12 about God's restoration in my family?

Am I willing to emulate the Great Gardener?

- Am I an affectionate and hands-on parent, willing to engage and show grace when my kids disappoint me as much as when they please me?
- What are the characteristics and actions of the Gardener's (the Father's) love in John 15 and Hosea 11?
- How do my practical priorities show that I place my children ahead of my career and personal pursuits?
- Do I prune each child according to his or her nature, or do I have a one-style-fits-all approach?

CHAPTER 2

EACH SAPLING ACCORDING TO ITS NATURE

In this chapter:

- What is temperament, and why should we understand it?
- How deep-rooted is temperament?
- A biblical foundation for temperament.
- The what, how, where, and why of parenting according to temperament.
- An introduction to the Tall Trees Kids Profile.

When I conveniently forget my past gardening failures and bravely venture into horticulture, I usually scan the nursery near our home for "easy plants"—those that basically don't need me to remember I have them! Their attractiveness matters, but I mostly look at the labels. What do they say? Full sun, or semishade? How often do I need to water the plants? If I buy several, how far apart should I plant them? If I look at getting a tree, how tall will it grow?

I do this for two reasons. I want to know how to care for the plants so they don't wither and die, and I want to know what to expect when they are grown—fruit, flowers, runners that will take over the entire garden?

Can you see that a plant's label is not a bad thing? It doesn't limit the plant in any way. It doesn't emphasize what the plant *can't* be. It only highlights the plant's innate potential and the ways in which I can nurture it into a flourishing shrub or tree.

WHAT IS TEMPERAMENT, AND WHY SHOULD WE UNDERSTAND IT?

Temperament is such a positive label. When I understand my child's innate design, I'm better equipped to answer these two pertinent questions:

1. How can I love you best?
2. What are reasonable expectations as you grow into adulthood?

The only thing more difficult than shaping a sapling is shaping a whole garden full of different saplings. Gardening quickly becomes like a journey through a jungle! Parents with more than one child sometimes get confused when they treat different saplings in the same way; one may bounce back while the other snaps under the pressure. For example, two children can be given an identical consequence—let's say, being sent to their rooms—for watching a program they're not allowed to watch. One may stay in the room, depressed and sulking for hours on end, while the other may come up with something fun to do within five minutes, unfazed.

Somewhere between what we do as parents and what our young saplings make of our actions, something wonderful and unpredictable happens. We don't always get the results we expect. Most of the time we get the opposite. But sometimes, to our astonishment, we get something much better than we deserve. Part of this mystery is the fact that temperament—our children's and our own—plays a much bigger role in the dynamics of parenting than we often wish to admit.

When parents do not understand their own temperaments, or those of their children, they can feel confused and frustrated. When they communicate poorly, rub each other the wrong way, and act in a way that is insensitive to each other's needs, a good relationship becomes almost impossible. These things happen just because we can't figure out what makes the other person tick.

Parents with more than one child often testify to the fact that their children were different even before birth—one was restless; the other one calm. As babies, one was greedy and quick; the other was lazy and contented. As toddlers, one was a screamer and the other a whiner. As teenagers, one was happy to stay home, while the other was the center of attraction at each and every party. Learning what these unique traits mean can make the difference between a difficult parenting experience and a rewarding one.

HOW DEEP-ROOTED IS TEMPERAMENT?

I believe temperament is the innate tendency to develop in a certain way. It determines, among other things, a person's likelihood of focusing on people or tasks, his or her budding as an introvert or extrovert, pessimist or optimist, thinker or talker, spectator or participant, leader or follower, individual or team player, agent of change or defender of the status quo, fighter or peacemaker. Temperament even predicts stress-management styles and one's perspective on success.

I consider temperament to be the soul's DNA. If one were to ignore temperament and raise all children the same, they could still display similar acquired behavior, but their spontaneous nature would still differ greatly. Let's say you teach your children to put away their belongings after playtime. The kids may be equally neat, but one group may achieve this by blackmailing their brothers or sisters to help tidy up, while the second group may think of ingenious ways to hide dirty laundry or toys. The third group may put everything away perfectly in its proper place, while the fourth group may keep everything neat from the onset so that cleaning up is easy and simple. The natural way in which each child rises to the expectations of the parent will remain unique.

As parents, we can try to change a child's natural temperament by molding a silly clown into a serious student or a shy wallflower into a student-body president, but they will be like tea bags—in hot water their true nature will come out. The silly clown will still show his red nose during stressful exam times, and the student-body president may need a few tearful minutes alone after her best speech to overanalyze what she could have said differently. Children will "remember" who they are subconsciously, and that basic nature will show up again and again in life, because it is inborn.

Below are two examples that show the necessity of knowing and cherishing the temperament of each of our children. They also illustrate how our own temperaments can trip us up when we assume that our children must think and behave the same way we do.

Example one: Two peace-loving parents lift up the baby blanket and there lies a wiggly, biting, obstinate little girl. They are scared and worried. However, they manage to keep her under control with discipline and, later in life, some medication to suppress her apparent hyperactivity and occupational therapy. They are very happy with the shape of their well-behaved, contented specimen. The moment she breaks away from their house and restraints, however, she bounces back to her own shape—rebellious and wild—and they can't understand why. They have overlooked the essence of this young tree. They shaped her in a way that left her original weak spots intact alongside a few acquired strengths that aren't even really hers.

If these parents had understood her nature, developed her positive traits, and improved on the challenging ones with compassion, then the outcome more than likely would have been a well-rounded, unique character. Her busy nature quite possibly could have developed into productivity and versatility, her hot-temperedness into determination and healthy competitiveness, and her obstinacy into creative leadership. Who knows?

Example two: Two driven, top-achieving parents lift up the baby blanket and there lies a contented bundle of peace. They can't believe how much he can sleep! He walks too slowly. He doesn't show enough interest in his surroundings. Eventually they get the little guy going with a firm shove and threats, and by enrolling him in every conceivable extracurricular activity. He complains that everything is boring and becomes pathetic when they push him too hard. After forcing him to do rugby, swimming, drama, gymnastics, and a foreign-language course, he announces he only wants to play chess. They're astonished that he doesn't want to be in the top ten of his class. How can somebody be happy with a C-average report card?

If only these parents had known what that sleepiness and contentment meant, they could have realized that this son of theirs would not have many passions in life. They could have wasted less time and money on activities that seemed meaningful to *them*. They would have known how debilitating to him the effects of their pressure were. They would have discovered the one thing he could focus on and excel at. Who knows what he would have achieved in life had they learned sooner to support him in that one thing—chess!

A BIBLICAL FOUNDATION FOR TEMPERAMENT

Train up a child in the way he should go, even
when he is old he will not depart from it.
Proverbs 22:6 NASB

Proverbs 22:6 is not a promise that children raised in church will all go to heaven. How I wish it were! It is a promise that children trained according to the way that God has for them will not become lost in life. The phrase "in the way" used here is the word *dar·kōw*, which Strong's Concordance defines as "the way" or "journey."[2] It sometimes refers to God's way but more often indicates a man's way or journey, and even the evil plans of some (1 Kings 8:32). In that sense, it encourages parenting that takes into account a child's unique life path.

According to the notes of renowned Bible scholar Albert Barnes, "in the way he should go" can also be translated "according to the tenor of his way," as the Darby Translation of the Bible words this verse. Barnes writes:

> *The way he should go—or, according to the tenor of his way, i.e., the path especially belonging to, especially fitted for, the individual's character. The proverb enjoins the closest possible study of each child's temperament and the adaptation of "his way of life" to that.*[3]

A root word of *dar·kōw* is *derek*, which means "way, road, distance, journey, manner,"[4] as it appears in Proverbs 22:6 of the Orthodox Jewish Bible: "Train up a na'ar in the derech [road] he should go, and when he is old, he will not depart from it."

In his book *Different Children, Different Needs*, Charles Boyd explains how this interpretation by some scholars has led him to believe that we as parents should indeed ask ourselves: How is my child put together on the inside, and what does that predict about the life direction that he should follow? How should I raise him in the light of this?[5]

I fully agree with the wording in the Amplified and Amplified Bible Classic Edition translations:

> *Train up a child in the way he should go [teaching him to seek God's wisdom and will for his abilities and talents], even when he is old he will not depart from it. (AMP)*

Train up a child in the way he should go [and in
keeping with his individual gift or bent], and when he
is old he will not depart from it. (AMP CLASSIC)

These perspectives confirm my conviction that each sapling emerges from mom's womb already bent in a certain way, and it can be dangerous if we try to "straighten" that natural bent according to our preferences. We run the risk of permanently damaging our sapling's character. By doing so, we can easily break its branches and confuse the child's sense of identity.

In both the Old Testament and the New Testament, the Lord announces births and gives parents the children's names and callings (*derek*) at the same time so they can cooperate with the Lord in shaping their children according to each child's unique purpose. It was not uncommon for parents to receive instructions beforehand on how to raise each of their children uniquely.

In the story of Samson's birth in Judges 13, we read that the Angel of the Lord gave detailed instructions to Samson's mother about her and Samson's diet, as well as his hair and also his purpose: he would begin the deliverance of Israel from the hands of the Philistines (verse 5). Verse 8 tells us: "Then Manoah prayed to the LORD: 'Pardon your servant, Lord. I beg you to let the man of God you sent to us come again to teach us how to bring up the boy who is to be born'" (NIV). It seems to me as if Manoah wanted firsthand instructions—he also wished for a manual! In verse 12 Manoah asked: "When your words are fulfilled, what is to be the rule that governs the boy's life and work?" (NIV). He was to have a unique child with a unique calling, and he wanted to do what would be most appropriate. Why should we settle for anything less?

We cannot change the nature of our saplings by forcing and fiddling with them. We will not get a Samson if we grow our son's hair. Grasshopper-and-honey sandwiches will not produce a second John the Baptist. We also won't be able to change our children's life course. We will, however, be able to make it more difficult or easier for them to find their passion, path, and purpose. We cannot change their inherent character, but we can impede or improve the development of their expression of that character. The Lord shapes the inside, and our task is to help the outside to match by disciplining in a way that suits each child's nature.

In later chapters we will investigate in more detail how the Lord deals with His individual children in different ways that align with their natures. We can gain a lot from these examples and also recognize in them the biblical mandate for adapting the way we handle our children according to their unique natures.

THE WHAT, HOW, WHERE, AND WHY OF PARENTING

Proverbs 22:6 deserves a closer look, because the what, the how, the where, and the why of parenting and discipline are implied in it.

What: train a child.

What does parenting entail? The phrase "train a child" is exactly what parenting is. Our instruction is not to control our child, but rather to prepare our child for adulthood by training him.

We will have to go through a lot of training sessions with our child. Think of a vine. It is "trained" to crawl up a trellis by putting support in place and by binding the tender stems to the supports. It's pruned by cutting out wayward growth. The result is a good harvest, and good wine or sweet table grapes. Parenting is similar. We guide firmly and use restraints to help a plant grow toward its full potential. Painful pruning is applied to willful defiance. It means that we ought to create opportunities to teach our children everything from table manners to sound financial principles through intentional exercises. We can't leave the learning to chance any more than a winemaker can hope the vine will grow upward by itself.

How: in the way he should go.

The phrase "in the way he should go" is the method. "Training" our children according to a strategic fertilizer regimen simplifies parenting. Each fruit tree has its own ideal pruning pattern, soil, and harvest time. And each has typical pests that need controlling. We can follow guidelines particular to each tree to prevent frostbite and to shield the young trees from overexposure, just as we do with young saplings. They also need enough of life's realities—wind, sun, and rain—to become mature.

If we have a child who finds it difficult to sit still in church and who needs lots of challenges, we can venture a guess that he won't be the kind of adult to sit still and accept the way things are. He is already showing us "his way"—active exploration. Training *him* in the way he should go probably shouldn't involve threats or bribes to get him to sit quietly, to page through a children's Bible, or to do puzzles. We'd do better to build in physical outlets before church and a surprise toy halfway through the service to keep him interested and occupied, as these resemble the strategies he will one day use to get through drawn-out meetings and to cope with situations that offer little in the way of excitement. Perhaps, for now, this young one is the ideal children's church candidate, as there he can practice the skills that come with his design (physical and enthusiastic participation) and the purpose he is likely made for (inspiring change).

Where: to the place from which he won't turn away.

Our primary responsibility as parents is to lead our children to Jesus, as He commands. From there we accompany and support them on the way to the places that the Lord will eventually reveal to them.

We can send our children toward the right destination only if we know what their natural, innate designs are. Few of us know this before their birth, and even in their infant years it may still be unclear, but if we pay close attention, we will soon be able to hazard a guess. Then we can work with the Lord in accompanying our children in fulfilling each one's life purpose, without which they won't be truly fulfilled.

Sooner or later, our children's temperaments will show us where they are going—some will become pioneers in unknown fields of science (revealed by their insatiable urge to explore, their daring nature, and their experimental curiosity). Others will follow careers of discipleship or service (revealed by their compassion for people, caring actions, and willingness to comply). Some are on their way to leadership (as we can already see from their constant hunger for control and their influence over others). Spectators who seldom set foot on the playing field of life when they are children will likely become philosophers and critical thinkers. We may not necessarily like the direction our children are going, but our task is not to choose that direction for them. We shouldn't underestimate the power of our own frame of reference. It can blind us to the value of our child's life purpose when it differs a great deal from our own!

Why: so when he is old he will not turn from it.

How do people lose direction in life? Remember, this scripture does not refer to the way to heaven. It refers to the way your child will go according to the direction indicator God has created in him. People lose their way if they ignore their direction indicator long enough. Not only that, but they may also lose their identity, their zest for life, their faith in the meaning of life, and all their joie de vivre.

The loss of one's inborn direction is similar to the loss of magnetism. A compass needle points to the magnetic north in the same way our temperament points us toward our life's calling. When other people rub us the wrong way with their "strong magnets," we can become "demagnetized." They may do this by saying that we could not possibly want to be the way we are and by insisting that we change. Many people have become paralyzed in exactly this way.

As parents, we try our best. We don't crush and disfigure our saplings on purpose. Many parents believe that saplings are broken by strict discipline and punishment. I believe it happens in many different ways, whenever our actions—including unreasonable punishment—deny, or attempt to distort, the innate nature of our child. Unfortunately, we sometimes unknowingly do this because we have an ideal in mind; we may think that there is such a thing as a perfect tree (perfect child, perfect wife, or perfect husband).

> *Let us beware and beware and beware of having an ideal for our children. So doing we damn them.*
>
> D. H. Lawrence, *Fantasia of the Unconscious*

Of course, children lose their way not only by pursuing the wrong callings but also by being on the wrong moral track in life. Every child's innate weaknesses reveal the most likely temptations that could make him lose his way. If we discipline our children with this perspective in mind, they will be more steadfast and resilient than children who were raised according to a standard "training program." We may have learned that our daughter's temperament puts her at risk of sexual experimentation; therefore, we pay more attention to her clothing, friends, and movie role models than to her math score. Or maybe our child, owing to his temperament, tends to twist the truth as a way of keeping his image as perfect as possible in the eyes of other people. We will emphasize the far more serious consequences of breaching someone's trust than making a few spelling mistakes in an essay. Building their defenses in the areas of their greatest vulnerability will do far more good than ticking off a list of "good" behaviors.

The ideal outcome of parenting is, therefore, so much more than just teaching children to follow their parents' example meekly. Instead, the aim should be to accompany children on their God-given paths so they might reach their own best destinations. God's plan for us and our children is ultimately for us to follow Him, and to encourage the generations down the line to do the same. If we drag our children with us on our course, we can take them further away from what God planned for them and miss the important teaching moments that are unique to their journeys. Their paths have to differ from ours because God doesn't clone people. A more detailed study of our own and our children's temperaments will help us tremendously in understanding this, and that is what the rest of this book will focus on.

AN INTRODUCTION TO THE TALL TREES KIDS PROFILE

I have created a personality indicator loosely based on the four-fold classification of Hippocrates because it has been researched throughout the ages, because many esteemed sources support it, and because several existing profiles correspond to it in principle. I have also studied personality, behavioral, and learning styles, because these are visible expressions of our invisible temperament. My colleague at Tall Trees, Annatjie van Zyl, contributed many insights through her own research. We have tested the profiles on many children over the years and are convinced that they add to the understanding of our saplings' beautiful inherent designs. The culmination of our combined research is the Tall Trees Kids Profile, which uses temperament characteristics and behavioral traits to identify four distinct "tree types," which can combine to form ten more hybrid tree types.

Understanding the four basic temperament types (chapters 4–7) will be enough for the parent who only wants to know how to handle a practical situation with a difficult two-year-old or "mold back into shape" a maverick tween. However, more than two-thirds of our children are combination types, hence the description of these "hybrid trees" in chapter 9.

I based this temperament profile on four tree types—a palm tree, a rose bush, a boxwood tree (sometimes called a topiary or lollipop tree), and a pine tree—because trees represent life, growth, potential, and beauty. Rose bushes come in many varieties, as do palm trees, boxwood trees, and pine trees. I want to acknowledge that we and our children can be unique and surprisingly different even within our types. Two pine trees may seem dissimilar because one exhibits only half of the characteristics of a pine tree while the other exhibits the other half of the typical traits.

When working with temperament indicators, there is no ideal profile. I disagree with books that encourage anyone to prefer a "well-rounded" profile that includes all four basic personalities. I do, however, agree that we should all take our weak points to Jesus so that His character can become more visible in us. He changes us through His Spirit as He sees fit by affording us the right opportunities to be shaped according to our purpose. We won't necessarily learn what we want, but what the Lord deems essential.

Sanctification through the Holy Spirit is not the same as equalization. We won't all become alike and representative of an "ideal person." Quite the opposite happens: we become "holier" in the sense that we become even more clearly "set apart"—each for a special purpose. Maturity then becomes the state in which our true selves emerge with fewer of the natural weaknesses and more of the natural strengths, operating in a way that blesses others and glorifies God.

Thus, the ideal temperament for each person is the temperament that best suits that person's purpose in life. And by the grace of God, we don't need to design this—we have received it as a gift. To be a "type" is not a bad thing if you are exactly the right "type" for the task at hand! Our innate temperaments find expression in sincere character—our own and that of our young saplings.

CHAPTER 3

THEIR OWN KIND OF NATURAL

In this chapter:

- The purpose of Tall Trees Profiles.
- The responsible way to use the profiles.
- The Tiny Trees Baby and Toddler Profile.
- Special notes for parents with toddlers.
- The Tall Trees Kids Profile.
- The Tall Trees Parenting Profile.

Did you skip the introduction and chapters 1 and 2 because you only want to know which type of tree your child is? If you did, I strongly recommend that you go back and start reading from the beginning. No technique, strategy, or profile can help you discipline your child if your heart is not *with* your child. Children have to be fully convinced of their parents' unconditional commitment and love; otherwise, their behavior will become so problematic that no discipline or temperament-specific quick fix—however appropriate or clever it may be—will have the desired result.

Love is the melody of a happy family, and discipline is the harmony. Together they make beautiful music. Unless discipline springs from a well of loving commitment, the music will be off-key. Please read the first chapter to make sure that unconditional love is your focus and that your aim is better understanding—firstly so you can love better, and secondly so you can discipline wisely.

So this is my prayer: that your love will flourish and that you will not only love much but well. Learn to love appropriately. You need to use your head and test your feelings so that your love is sincere and intelligent, not sentimental gush.

Philippians 1:9–10

THE PURPOSE OF THE PROFILES

And isn't that what life is all about—the ability to go around back and to come up inside somebody else's mind, to look at the ... wonder and say: "Oh, so that's how you see it?! Well now, I must remember that!"

Ray Bradbury, *Dandelion Wine*

Before you complete the Tall Trees Kids Profile, please look at its aim again: the goal is to understand better so we can shape our saplings for their purpose. This background on temperament will give us perspective. In fact, perspective is what it is all about. We want to "enter" our children's heads, "look around" inside, and learn more about the way they experience life.

When you have completed the profile for each of your children and for yourself, the next step will be to read the chapter on each tree type that corresponds best with your children and you. It would be beneficial to familiarize yourself with all the tree types because we sometimes see our children from our own frames of reference. That is why it's so important to determine our own profiles as well! A slow child may seem even slower to a fast-paced parent, and a strong-willed parent will probably experience any resistance from his child more intensely.

Also, sometimes a child's true character develops slowly, or we are slow in getting to know our introverted child. Therefore, it is valuable to get to know all the tree types.

THE RESPONSIBLE WAY TO USE THE PROFILES

Please be mindful of the following guidelines:

- Guard against deciding beforehand which type of tree your children may be.
- You need not get upset if you recognize and have to select negative characteristics in your children. It's easier to identify weak points than strong points, and profiles that are approached in a "negative" manner are typically more accurate than those that use only strong points to evaluate.
- If possible, complete the profile with another adult who knows your child well. It will be more accurate than a one-sided score.

- Be careful not to get stuck on your child's prominent temperament type and forget that your sapling represents a unique blend of characteristics! Keep looking at your child with your eyes wide open, and keep listening with an attentive ear.

- Ensure that your child is healthy and happy when you take the profile. Recent trauma, illness, or a strained relationship with you can affect the outcome. Ensure your child knows that the purpose of the profile is to understand her and be a better parent to her.

- Repeat the profile every few months or at least annually. It is not a onetime psychometric test. Children often seem to change when new characteristics come to the fore as their young lives mature.

- Avoid using the tree-type label until your child knows enough about her strengths to carry the tree name with healthy pride and an appreciation for the strengths of others. Always use "Tree Talk" rather than critical ways when affirming.

- Remember that the guidelines given in the following chapters are only that—guidelines. They will help us if we lack confidence, wisdom, intuition, and insight. They should, however, never replace Spirit-led parenting. I trust God more with your family than I trust my own advice for you!

There are many characteristics that do not appear in the profiles. Any profile is a selection of characteristics that are typical and central to the personality type. Because they can never be exhaustive, it is possible to get an inaccurate or incomplete picture. The picture scenarios for the preschoolers to tweens and the indicators included in the profile tests for the babies and toddlers have been researched and clarified repeatedly. If, however, the score classifies your child as a particular tree but the description in the corresponding chapter or report doesn't feel right to you, there may be a rare mismatch between the test's specific combination of core characteristics and your child's combination of primary traits. Don't blindly follow the manual for that tree in such cases. Instead, read the chapter on each tree type and the hybrid trees to broaden your perspective until you feel you have a grip on who your child is and what she needs.

THE TINY TREES BABY AND TODDLER PROFILE

Temperament is present and programmed artfully even before birth.[6] If we know what to look for, we can sometimes recognize a baby's profile within days of birth. However, when it comes to children, parents can be too close to see clearly. Illness, allergies, hunger, and other disruptions can make babies act opposite to their nature too. Have a look at these descriptions of babies and toddlers under eighteen months. Perhaps relatives and caregivers can add their two cents to complete the picture!

The Rose Bush baby and toddler:

- wants to crawl, stand, and walk early
- dislikes being strapped in or confined
- is on the move—explores the world actively
- tries to master tasks alone
- won't lie still for a peaceful cuddle
- tries to play with older children
- has their first temper tantrum before age one
- is demanding and impatient
- screams with a purpose—to move others
- has a determined expression
- often resists hugs and kisses
- becomes upset when called "baby" or "small"
- plays more destructively or aggressively than others
- reacts fast and fiercely when hurt
- bites, hits, or screams at adults when frustrated
- won't give up or be distracted from what they want
- actively fights against sleep even when exhausted
- takes risks—seems fearless

The Palm Tree baby and toddler:

- coos and babbles early and constantly
- is distractible and easy to entertain
- is full of silliness and laughs
- plays with their own voice and reflection
- has bright, alert eyes

- easily trusts strangers
- laughs at your strict face when you scold them
- is very excitable
- loves intense cuddles
- cries when parents walk away
- is exceptionally curious to taste and touch things
- tries to be cute and charming
- enjoys imitating others and dressing up
- cannot play alone quietly
- copies rude words and actions for attention
- quickly bounces back after tears
- gets hyper and acts silly when tired
- wiggles body and limbs wildly when impatient

The Pine Tree baby and toddler:

- enjoys watching people
- is contented and quiet
- sleeps more than other children their age
- isn't driven to master new skills
- is patient while being changed or fed
- is comforted by a familiar, friendly face
- becomes upset when overstimulated
- seems to be disinterested and dreamy
- avoids strangers, noise, and movement
- doesn't explore their surroundings actively
- is lazy to start walking does not cry, laugh, or "talk" much

- drinks, eats, or reacts slowly
- melts into tears when scolded
- enjoys gentle touches
- grows attached to a sensory-soothing object or toy
- gives up quickly when effort is required
- loves other babies and baby animals

The Boxwood Tree baby and toddler:

- has a soft, whimpering cry
- is careful and uncertain in new settings
- likes a fixed routine
- is seldom naughty, usually well behaved
- gets very upset about accidents
- senses boundaries and dangers
- can fall asleep alone after a gentle bedtime routine
- can play alone for long periods of time
- cries or "complains" about other kids
- often looks sad
- is sensitive to changes in surroundings
- is fussy—needs things to be "just right"
- demands a lot of comfort and care
- whines when tired and often wakes up irritated
- seems to enjoy learning new things
- loves books, stories, songs, and rhymes
- takes a long time to settle down after being upset or hurt
- wants to be the parents' little helper

SPECIAL NOTES TO PARENTS OF TODDLERS

Almost all parents of two- or three-year-olds think their saplings are Rose Bushes. This is often a "false Rose Bush phase" (which can reoccur in the late teens). The will is strong at these ages, emotions are out of control, and language development is not adequate to express complex needs and feelings. Outbursts are the order of the day. In this phase of development, children start to form independence and an identity. They will start pulling away from you to explore their own influence on their surroundings. What may seem like disobedience is in fact a necessary developmental milestone! It is the worst time to try to determine your child's profile accurately, but it is also the time when you most need guidelines for your child.

Here are a few ways to get a clearer picture of your toddler's tree type at this stage:

For one week, make notes of the type of outbursts your toddler has.
Typical Rose Bush: Rage and violence—intense and long lasting. The outburst feels like an intentional attack on you and elicits your anger. It is the typical temper tantrum, usually brought on by something you did or expected your child to do that didn't suit him, or by you saying no to your child.

Typical Palm Tree: Melodrama (acting)—stops when your child is ignored. The tears are soon forgotten. Sometimes the outburst is comical and totally out of proportion to the situation. It leaves you confused, surprised, and sometimes even smiling! It is usually targeted at keeping your attention focused on your child.

Typical Pine Tree: Refusal and helplessness—this reaction won't register on the Richter scale like the outburst of the Rose Bush, because it happens quietly. The little one just doesn't want to cooperate and becomes paralyzed and stubborn as a last resort. Your child turns into a helpless, motionless bundle. You feel discouraged, impatient, or frustrated.

Typical Boxwood: Nags and moans—this, too, is a prolonged outburst, more draining than intense. It frazzles and exhausts you. It seems as if your child can't shake the feeling. It is often triggered by something that hurt or disappointed your child. Your child seems more unhappy or overwhelmed than angry.

Jot down the message your baby's or toddler's actions convey most in the course of a week. Find the description below that agrees most with your child's early words and behavior.

Typical Rose Bush: No! I will! *Now!* I can do it myself! Leave me alone! I won! Mine!

Typical Palm Tree: Look here! Come here! Look at me! Play with me! Wow! Hurrah!

Typical Pine Tree: I don't want to. I can't. Help me! Wait for me! I'm too tired. I'm too small.

Typical Boxwood: I'm scared! I don't like it! It hurts! It's not nice! It's wrong! I feel sick!

For one week, observe the way your child plays.

Typical Rose Bush: Orders friends around, makes the rules, fights, competes, bullies, grabs, kicks, bites, tries to do everything quicker, higher, or better. Gets angry when things don't go their way. Play can get rough and dangerous.

Typical Palm Tree: Doesn't want to play alone. Prefers people to toys. Plays silly, imaginative, exuberant, and noisy games. Alternates quickly between different activities and toys. Easily gets bored with one thing, place, or friend.

Typical Pine Tree: Plays more "next to" friends than with them. Does not enjoy sharing toys and would rather be left to do their own thing. Pulls away from rough play. Responds to cries and needs of friends, though, and acts very caring toward them.

Typical Boxwood: Likes playing alone, in a corner, or with one friend. Gets upset when others do something wrong, break a toy, or threaten their personal space. Plays for hours on end with one thing—usually indoors, but when outside, plays mostly in one spot. Avoids noisy, rough friends. Can follow simple rules of a game from a very young age.

Pay attention to the types of circumstances that upset your child most.

Typical Rose Bush: confinement and the word *no*.

Typical Palm Tree: loneliness, hunger, and boredom.

Typical Pine Tree: overstimulation as a result of a very busy day or a long time in a busy environment.

Typical Boxwood: discomfort (for example, too hot or too cold) or unpredictable circumstances.

After a week, these observations should shed some light on your toddler's true tree type. If they do not, read the manuals again, especially following the advice for a Rose Bush, and repeat the profile in six months' time. You can still parent well without the label!

THE TALL TREES KIDS PROFILE

At Evergreen Parenting and Tall Trees Profiles, we are constantly refining the profiles and temperament tests for adults and children. The latest versions are available at talltreestraining.com. To access one free individualized, in-depth Tall Trees Kids Profile Report, find the scratch-away code on the back cover of this book, then follow the instructions on the Kids Profile Test page under the Products menu at talltreestraining.com. Taking the test is free for all readers of *Growing Kids with Character*. You have the option to purchase additional individualized reports at a discount for your other children. The directions to unlock this optional discount are given where you access the Kids Profile.

After taking the test and accessing the Tall Trees Kids Profile, your child's result will direct you to the relevant chapters in this book. If your child's profile corresponds with one of the four tree types, you'll learn most of what you need from the chapters about that tree. If your child is a combination, you'll find it helpful to read all the chapters related to your child's result (for example, parents of Box-Pines should read both the Boxwood Tree and Pine Tree chapters) as well as the Box-Pine section in chapter 9, "Hybrid Trees." Your child could be a mix of three tree types! In that case, the result would be what we call a Contra Tree. Contra-Palm means every tree *except* Palm Tree; a Contra-Rose has Boxwood, Pine Tree, and Palm Tree characteristics; and so forth.

THE TALL TREES PARENTING PROFILE

Knowledge of temperament is like the oxygen mask in an airplane. When cabin pressure is lost, you ought to put on your own mask before assisting your children! We see our kids through the tinted lenses of our own tree types, so it is helpful to know what our tree types are.

You can determine your tree type for free by completing the Tall Trees Parenting Profile on the same website or app noted above. You can obtain a free result by following the directions on the site or app for a free test.

You will receive your instant result on screen and by email so you can always revisit your result, and the purchase of the complete individualized report is optional. (Note that purchasing my book *(un)Natural Mom* gives you a discount on this individualized parent report and contains more details about each type of mother or father.)

CHAPTER 4

PARENTING THE PALM TREE

Read this chapter if your child tested Palm Tree, Box-Palm, Palm-Rose, Pine-Palm, or a combination of Palm Tee, Rose Bush, and Pine Tree called a Contra-Boxwood, as it is a mixture of every tree except Boxwood Tree. These trees are all in the Palm Tree family. Also read chapter 9 if your child is not a "pure" Palm Tree.

In this chapter:

- Meet Ruth, a natural Palm Tree.
- Develop—how to nurture the nature of a young Palm Tree.
- Direct—what and how to teach a Palm Tree.
- Dialogue—how to speak the Palm Tree dialect.
- Discipline—how to train the Palm Tree way.
- Disciple—how to shape the Palm Tree's character for God's purpose.

To appreciate this tree type, you need to visualize a palm tree on an island—with coconuts hanging from the tree, ready to drop onto someone's head, and monkeys playing around in the branches, ready for mischief. When the island music plays and the hula girls sway to and fro in their grass skirts, the palm trees sway in unison with them. They are at the center of every beach party. Etched against the sunset, they make us long for the next weekend or holiday. They are jovial, fun-loving trees far removed from the seriousness the rest of us possess. They proclaim from the rooftops, "Live for the moment! Enjoy the sun! Life is a feast!"

Palm Trees do not change much as they grow. The lower fronds dry up and the trunks grow taller, but the waving treetops stay the same. People with this temperament keep their childlikeness, joie de vivre, and sparkle to their dying day. In a certain sense they also just grow taller (and their toys get more expensive!). They can seem surprising, weird, and wonderful, from a different planet. They bring color to black-and-white situations, and their over-the-top humor can sometimes leave us gasping for breath.

MEET RUTH, A NATURAL PALM TREE

Ruth is the eight-year-old daughter of Pine Tree mom Penny.

Ruth's curly hair and bright eyes remind one of a comic-strip character. When she was four, her giggles and screams elicited regular knocking on the very thin walls between her parents' apartment and the neighbors'. Her parents didn't have the heart to ask her straight out to turn down the volume, because she was just too adorable. They were also wrapped around her candy-sticky little finger, as they felt too sorry for her to really get upset with her. Everyone just accepted that she was loud! Ruth's baby photos showed pink gums and eyes crinkling with laughter. Her first word was "Wow!" Flipping through her baby album shows the astonishing number of her performances that were captured on film. There was the day when she decorated herself with Daddy's shaving cream to "look like Santa Claus." Then there was the beautiful photo of the time when she stormed onto the stage during her older sister's school concert and started meowing with the cats into the microphone—complete with claws bared at the sides of her face.

One day Ruth got hold of her mom's makeup, and when she was done with her face, she looked as if she had been in a serious accident. Ruth thought she was so beautiful that it was difficult to get her away from the mirror!

When Ruth is told to put away toys, it usually leads to another game or a long story. "The balls just told me they would rather sleep in the garden because it is too hot in the house." If that doesn't work, she becomes a character. "I'm a frog now. Frogs can't see what blocks are." Whenever her father has had enough of these delay tactics and raises his voice, she bursts out laughing at the serious face. This, of course, adds fuel to the fire. If Dad explodes, Ruth breaks into heart-wrenching sobs, and Penny has to come to the rescue. Mom cleans up the mess in the name of love and for the sake of sanity. It works every time. Ruth's tears quickly dry up, and she runs off to wreak havoc elsewhere.

Ruth gets invited to the birthday parties of everyone in her class and secretly is the favorite grandchild of both sets of grandparents. She loves sharing hugs and kisses and says the cutest things.

At school, though, it's a different story. When she was halfway through first grade, her parents received a shocking report: Ruth's task orientation was below average for her age. She didn't complete tasks, and her attention wandered. The school recommended that she be evaluated for attention deficit disorder and hyperactivity, and her teacher saw her as a good candidate for medication. Ruth's parents were in a state over this. They know she is intelligent and creative. Why does she struggle with her schoolwork?

Ruth's jovial nature allows her to get away with murder at times. She uses flattery, and her smile gets even the most hardened slave drivers to lower their standards to a level that she can reach. As she gets older, she will probably hand in assignments late, forget her sports gear at home, and lose a pair of shoes at least once a year; but she'll explain everything so well that those who listen to her will clearly understand it wasn't her fault.

When Ruth starts junior high school, her father could have a hard time. The big challenge comes as Palm Tree hormones kick in. It won't even help to buy the proverbial shotgun to keep the young men at bay, because Ruth won't necessarily bring them home. It may be the boys who need protecting. She will probably spend a lot of time away from home, hanging out elsewhere with a large group of friends. Her social needs may seem excessive to her parents, and they may lie awake many a night wondering what she is up to, praying she'll be able to resist peer pressure and the urge to do everything that feels good.

There are also the issues of hair, clothing, and jewelry. With a Palm Tree, one should expect a colorful journey to self-discovery!

People will probably say many of these things to her someday:

- "You are the life of the party."
- "Nothing gets you down."
- "You are an adrenaline junkie."
- "You can sell sand to an Arab living in the desert and ice to an Eskimo living in an igloo."
- "Can't you ever think before acting?"
- "Aren't you ever serious?"
- "What's your latest scheme?"

DEVELOP — HOW TO NURTURE THE NATURE OF A YOUNG PALM TREE

In your child's Tall Trees Kids Profile Report, his or her unique set of needs will be listed as the Palm Tree's "Fertilizer."

1. Applause and the spotlight: If the families of young Palm Trees don't appreciate them, they may go after the approval of others, often with disastrous consequences. We'd be wise to applaud the loudest and give the most attention if we want to keep our Palm Trees close to us! Allow them to perform, and reward them with age-appropriate certificates, medals, trophies, and other visible proofs of success for everything they achieve. Who says we can't celebrate their first permanent tooth or first pimple while we're at it! Use any milestone as an opportunity to show them that you're paying attention.

2. Lots of hugs, kisses, touching, and pampering: Palm Trees are very aware of their senses and *feel* love much better than they can *hear* it! Sometimes they just want to be tickled, wrestled with, or given a pat on the back. But their need for physical contact stays with them throughout their teens. Because these saplings are most likely to get involved in physical relationships with the opposite sex,

we give them a valuable advantage when we fulfill this physical need with constant affection.

Baby girls are picked up, played with, cuddled, and kissed about five times as much as baby boys (which could explain why so many young boys have five times more learning and behavioral problems than young girls). The younger the boy, the more he needs this pampering. Boys need hugs until they are at least seven or eight years old, and after that they obviously need other forms of touching, such as wrestling. Parents tend to pamper their children less and less as they get older. However, girls' need for physical contact, especially with their fathers, peaks at eleven![7]

3. Acceptance of unusual characteristics, ideas, and behaviors: Palm Trees often become pioneers, inventors, and explorers thanks to their curiosity and unique perspectives. If we fuel their strange ideas rather than extinguish them, we might be doing the whole world a favor.

At age three, Palm Tree Liam refused to go to school wearing matching shoes. Always a flip-flop on one foot and a rain boot on the other. After a week of this, his mom got a few messages from some frustrated mothers saying that their sons also wanted to wear this new mismatching-shoe style to school. This trendsetter Palm Tree was operating in his gifting—influencing people!

4. Humor and a positive attitude: Palm Trees can't handle pessimism well. They tend to flee a home where the atmosphere is serious and negative. They will also withdraw if treated with too much criticism and suspicion. It works better to broach serious subjects with a joke rather than a long face.

You can use fun games, rhymes, or songs to teach Palm Tree preschoolers table manners and how to do tedious chores, such as tidying up. Our family had a pink plastic pig who addressed bad manners at the dinner table. His name was Oh-Oh. If someone chewed with an open mouth or put his knife in his mouth, the one who first noticed this could put Oh-Oh in front of the guilty party's plate. Instead of announcing bath time with a watch in your hand, you could make a face and say, "I can smell it's bath time for someone's feet!"

5. Flexible structure and routine: Because Palm Trees are not naturally bound to time and order, it makes little sense to link routine events like bath time and bedtime strictly to the clock. One should rather focus on the sequence: Before you can watch television, you must first tidy your room; as soon as you have finished eating, it's time to brush your teeth. Change up chores now and then to give Palm Trees the variety they crave. My Palm Tree friend claims she loses all her creativity because of what she calls "routinitis"—a condition she has on weekdays when she needs to operate on the clock. Your young Palm Tree can possibly identify.

6. Opportunities to be creative and original: This means telling them what to do but leaving how to do it up to them. If a Palm Tree decides not to make his bed in the traditional way today but rather to roll up his blankets and sheets like sausages and arrange them in a row on the bed, let it be. At least the bedding is not strewn on the floor! Also, give him the opportunity to develop his entrepreneurial skills and natural sales talent.

7. Fun and laughter: The way to a Palm Tree's heart is through fun. Our relationships with them depend on our ability to accommodate this. We simply have to make time to take part in their favorite activities when they ask us to, or allow them to go and play, play, play—in an appropriate environment, of course. Facilitate fun

under your own roof so you can supervise these kids yourselves (and consequently become familiar with the quickest route to the ER).

8. Fantasy: This need is especially prominent in young Palm Trees. They want to hear lots and lots of stories and have your attention when they tell you about their own adventures—especially those that never really happened. Don't pass these off as fibs or punish them for telling tall tales until they're nine or ten. Rather, tell them that you enjoy their stories, appreciate their jokes, and love their interesting tales.

Five-year-old Sjanica is the proud owner of a large imagination, always making her own world more exciting. Old songs get new rhythms and lyrics. She can give a silly creature—a combination of a shopping cart, opossum, and cockatoo—a species name in seconds. She drew a makeshift person on her car seat, and when her mom asked why she had drawn on her chair, she answered without batting an eye, "So I won't be lonely. Now I have a friend!"

9. Time to be social: Palm Trees get snappy and negative when they don't spend time with friends. They also thrive on family vacations, playdates, and other gatherings. They practice their God-given people skills at these events. This is their way of getting to know themselves—by seeing their reflection in other people's eyes. We'll delay their journey to adulthood if we keep them cooped up.

Sjanica keeps telling her parents that she's nervous she won't make any friends. Meanwhile, her teacher says she's a popular girl who has several friends in her own grade and older friends wrapped around her little finger. She calls herself "Snuggle Bug" and lives up to her title: ten minutes into a new friendship and she's dishing out hugs.

10. A stimulating environment and action: Palm Trees begin to act up when they get bored. Their attention span is usually short, and they dislike sitting still for long periods or being subjected to one compulsory activity.

On her first day of first grade, Carli expected "big school" to be an exciting place. As she hopped into the car after school, though, her face fell. "Mom, I was so excited! But everyone is wearing the same dresses and shorts. Everyone looks the same, Mom! It's a mess. I can't find anybody because they all look the same. And the playground is way too small. I want to go back to kindergarten; there's more play space there. You know, Mom, if you were me, you'd be just as confused and frustrated. That many children makes a person feel hopeless, Mom. So, I just sat on the ledge and watched everyone else play." She sighed and finished with, "It's the day I've been waiting for, for *years*, but now I'm just looking forward to putting on different clothes *after* school."

11. Permission to be passionate: Palm Trees come up with many far-out pursuits. When a Palm Tree is determined to shatter the world record in water treading, it's difficult to share his enthusiasm, but if he doesn't constantly have something to get excited about, his passion for life could grow faint. We should make an effort to fan this enthusiasm rather than smother the flame. The next bandwagon is on its way!

12. Space to experiment with their physical appearance: Palm Tree preschoolers love television characters and superheroes. The boys may want to live in their Superman outfits for weeks on end. The girls also choose role models and fashion their hair or clothes accordingly. In their tween years, they start experimenting wildly with fashion and

personal style. We can speed up the process by waiting patiently, or delay it by giving negative feedback on every experiment.

DIRECT — WHAT AND HOW TO TEACH A PALM TREE

Our Palm Trees have to be trained:

1. To spend (and save!) money and time sensibly: Palm Trees could start off with little money, early curfews, and short periods in front of the television or computer, then learn, step by step, how to be increasingly responsible with their time and money. They must be given more rope only after they have proved to be trustworthy and responsible. We train them for real life when we give them enough money to let them experience the thrill of the buy and the sting of being wasteful.

2. To persevere with boring chores: This is obviously very difficult if fun is their credo! Our efforts won't go to waste if we equip our Palm Trees with the necessary skills to triumph over boredom with perseverance. When Palm Trees are young, we can already teach them to turn chores into games and focus their attention on something pleasant while their hands are doing tedious tasks.

3. To take responsibility for their own duties: Palm Trees often subcontract other people to do undesirable work and solve their problems for them. Our son once said to his sister, "If you fetch my sandals from the jungle gym for me, I'll feel so good about you!" However, this behavior can become an integrity issue if we don't teach them that they may not use their charisma to shirk responsibility. There are times when they need to face the music themselves.

4. To defer satisfaction and wait their turn: Palm Trees can become impatient when they don't get attention immediately. It's always their turn. When their impulsiveness shows every now and again, remorse usually comes too late. We wish they could think before acting, and that is exactly what we need to teach them! Try to create opportunities where your Palm Trees have to wait. Don't place their breakfast in front of them the moment they open their eyes in the morning.

When they want to say something and you're on the phone, let them sit nearby on a "waiting mat" until you have finished talking. Give them your full attention as soon as you're ready.

Often play games that involve taking turns with your Palm Trees, as well as board or card games where even more frequent turns are taken.

When Palm Trees impulsively hurt other children who hurt them, have them sit out a few rounds and demand that they apologize before permitting them to rejoin the game.

Don't allow them to corner you with their impulsivity. When a Palm Tree storms into the room shouting, "I should have been there already! I am going to the movies with Anne, okay? Please say yes, please? The movie starts in ten minutes!" it is hard to put the brakes on the runaway train, but we have to do it. Urgency puts undue pressure on the parent. That is not the way to ask permission.

5. To be serious when necessary: We have probably all experienced Palm Trees who can ruin a quiet, serious atmosphere. What do they do just as the solemn sermon reaches its peak on a Sunday morning? They burp, or worse! They become unsettled by

seriousness. However, seriousness is a component of respect and must be acquired.

6. To practice skills and do chores, even when they aren't fun: Three-year-old Palm Tree Lizemarie refused to eat her oatmeal by herself and wanted her mom to feed it to her. Mom explained that to be a good mother she needed to let her daughter sit at the table and eat her own food. Lizemarie flopped onto the couch, wearing a dashing smile, and said, "Mommy, be a bad mommy and feed me!"

From an early age, these saplings must learn to complete age-appropriate chores before they can do any "fun" things. Expect your preschoolers to straighten their beds or put away their pajamas before they are allowed to start playing in the morning.

Be patient if they forget to do certain things. Instead of accusing them of not doing a good job, you may ask, "Can you think of one of your chores you still need to do?" Create visual clues that can help them remember, such as putting a picture of a dog on your child's door if she forgets to feed the dog.

7. To say no to peer pressure: Palm Tree preschoolers worship their parents as heroes. Then one day they decide their friends are their heroes, and the parents are ignorant and old fashioned. For this reason, you really must have the first basic chats about sex, drugs, pornography, alcohol, inappropriate movies, occult games, and other evils while you are still wonderful and clever in their eyes.

Challenge your Palm Tree to apply his influence and convictions positively. Ask questions such as, "What can you do to help your friends when someone dares them to lift up a girl's skirt?" or, "Who would you tell if you see a friend buy pills from someone?"

Have frequent debates about values, rules, and important life choices with your older Palm Tree child. To a yes-person like your Palm Tree, the no you want him to say will come only after much practice.

8. To think ahead and plan accordingly: If one is wired to live for the moment, planning ahead is painful, but we adults know how essential this skill is. Our Palm Trees will most likely become entrepreneurs. All the wonderful ideas will come to fruition only if we have taught our Palm Trees to plan for the future and see beyond the horizon. They can draw a simple picture plan or jot down broad strokes. For a Palm Tree, that's already something!

Our Palm Trees learn best:

- from experience, practice, and mistakes
- when there are real consequences for their actions
- by completing a task with someone else
- when the focus is on the positive
- when the destination and reward are within reach
- when their physical needs are addressed first
- when the parent talks less and does more
- when the lesson is short and sweet and has practical value
- when they can use all their senses
- when the parent uses humorous and everyday examples
- from a role model whom they admire

DIALOGUE — HOW TO SPEAK THE PALM TREE DIALECT

How does God speak to Palm Trees?

> *If you TELL a child to do something, expect obedience; if*
> *you ASK a child to do something, expect an opinion.*
>
> Ronald Morrish, *Secrets of Discipline for Parents and Teachers*

The apostle Peter was a classic Palm Tree, and we can learn a lot from these key passages where Jesus and Peter have two important conversations.

> *Jesus replied, "Blessed are you, Simon son of Jonah, for this was not*
> *revealed to you by flesh and blood, but by my Father in heaven.*
> *And I tell you that you are Peter, and on this rock I will build my*
> *church, and the gates of Hades will not overcome it. I will give you*
> *the keys of the kingdom of heaven; whatever you bind on earth will*
> *be bound in heaven, and whatever you loose on earth will be loosed*
> *in heaven." Then he ordered his disciples not to tell anyone that he*
> *was the Messiah. From that time on Jesus began to explain to his*
> *disciples that he must go to Jerusalem and suffer many things at the*
> *hands of the elders, the chief priests and the teachers of the law, and*
> *that he must be killed and on the third day be raised to life. Peter*
> *took him aside and began to rebuke him. "Never, Lord!" he said.*
> *"This shall never happen to you!" Jesus turned and said to Peter,*
> *"Get behind me, Satan! You are a stumbling block to me; you do not*
> *have in mind the concerns of God, but merely human concerns."*
> Matthew 16:17–23 NIV

When they had finished eating, Jesus said to Simon Peter, "Simon son of John, do you love me more than these?" "Yes, Lord," he said, "you know that I love you." Jesus said, "Feed my lambs." Again Jesus said, "Simon son of John, do you love me?" He answered, "Yes, Lord, you know that I love you." Jesus said, "Take care of my sheep." The third time he said to him, "Simon son of John, do you love me?" Peter was hurt because Jesus asked him the third time, "Do you love me?" He said, "Lord, you know all things; you know that I love you." Jesus said, "Feed my sheep."

John 21:15–17 NIV

Jesus uses Peter's name repeatedly to make sure He has his attention (John 21).

Jesus warns Peter against a carnal perspective and candidly points out his weaknesses (Matthew 16:23; John 18:11).

Jesus repeats important things that He wants Peter to grasp (John 21:15–19). Palm Trees are quick to answer and speak impulsively. Maybe that's why Jesus asked Peter three times whether he loved Him, because Jesus wanted an honest answer straight from the heart, not idle words.

Jesus blesses Peter, talks to him in colorful pictures, and gives him a vision for his future and calling (Matthew 16:17–19).

How should we talk to our Palm Trees?

Keep the following principles in mind to ensure your Palm Tree hears you:

Address Palm Trees directly. This means you have to say their name, even touch them while you speak, and expect them to answer you, "Yes, Dad. Yes, Mom." Palm Trees sometimes seem to have poor attention spans because they seldom do what you ask the first time around. Ask them to repeat the instruction you gave so that you can be certain they remember.

Use humor as often as possible. "I see you've tried to make your bedroom floor disappear! Please make it reappear before your friends come around" will work better than "Please clean up your mess before your friends see what a slob you are."

Communicate emotionally rather than rationally, and more personally than theoretically. For example, "I'm not surprised they chose you for the part! I'd love to be in a play with you too!" works better than "You deserved the role. You remembered your words and your impersonation was spot on." Keep it short, because most Palm Trees can focus for only a short while.

Require eye contact from Palm Trees while you speak, because they may very well be focused on something else already.

If you have to correct them, be honest but sensitive and do it in private. They want to save face.

Beware of a negative or sarcastic tone. Palm Trees hear every nuance, and should you raise your voice, they are likely to hear anger in your tone and completely miss the message.

Be expressive when praising Palm Trees. Be specific about the person rather than the achievement. "I can't tell you how much I enjoyed watching you play today! You played with such passion!" instead of "Your game was excellent. You made use of every opportunity because you were placed just right on the field."

Nothing lights up Palm Trees' enthusiasm quicker than statements such as, "It has never been done that way. It might be impossible. I would love to see you try."

In summary:

- Make positive contact.
- Be brief.
- Use humor.
- Make sure they heard you.
- Make a wonderful fuss of the results.

How can we listen to our Palm Trees better?

Lower yourself to their level, look them in the eyes, and touch them.

Listen with your whole body. Smile, react, comment, and laugh with them, and share your stories as well. They enjoy it when you align with their stories.

Enjoy their imagination. Understand their need to be colorful, and let the story entertain you even if the details aren't factually true.

Respect their ideas when they share their dreams with you. Be supportive, even if you think it's crazy.

Talking is like breathing to them. They need a sounding board. Therefore, try not to silence them unnecessarily. They easily experience this as rejection.

Listen carefully for manipulation, because these Palm Trees can masterfully disguise a sharp arrow aimed craftily at your soft spot. You need not get angry, but be firm when they start negotiating for an answer different from the one you've given.

Anyone who thinks the art of conversation is
dead ought to tell a child to go to bed.

Robert C. Gallagher, *Destiny: A Journey of Discovery and Awakening*

DISCIPLINE — HOW TO TRAIN THE PALM TREE WAY

Each tree type has its own pruning and watering needs. These approaches work the best with Palm Trees:

1. Distractions and alternatives: Their attention can be like a butterfly's path over flowers—only touching down, never really sitting tight. If a one-year-old is screaming at the top of his voice because you stopped him from eating the whole chocolate cake, you can possibly divert his attention by amusing him with a hand puppet and a funny voice.

If you must tell a Palm Tree, "You are not allowed to …" follow up with, "but you may …" Alternatives help Palm Trees make a better choice. If we don't offer a substitute, they will go back to the undesirable behavior, because they can't sit around doing nothing.

2. Physical consequences (pain or pleasure): Palm Trees are one of two tree types that react well to such consequences. They don't usually take it personally and don't feel offended. They definitely don't always obey after the first punishment, but with consistent follow-up, the lesson does dawn on them! Remember, they are optimists! They think, *Oh, she got me this time! It was merely bad luck. I'll have another go at it!*

Three-year-old Palm Tree Emil is an example of this optimism. He emptied a whole bottle of shampoo into the shower so he could skate around on the slippery surface. His mom remained calm, swiftly removed him to safety, then told him they wouldn't be able to make their usual weekly trip to buy candy, because they would have to use the treat money to replace the shampoo he poured out. He cried rivers, and she thought the lesson was learned. She replaced the shampoo, and sure enough, Emil enjoyed another slip-and-slide shower that very evening. It will clearly require a more painful consequence before he is willing to give up the new-found, dangerous thrill. His mom may decide that a spanking for repeating the "game" is warranted, as it could save him from serious injury.

When a form of discipline doesn't work the first time, parents too often regress to the only other weapon they can think of—shouting! These frustrated exclamations fall on deaf ears because Palm Trees are known to be hard of hearing. Loud appeals are of little value. Persevering with tangible consequences should really be our first choice. Tangible consequences include taking away treats (for another week, or three perhaps), removing their toys, restricting them to a boring spot, postponing playdates, switching off the entertainment screens, or canceling a fun outing.

Spanking has become unpopular, and not without reason. Unfortunately, many adults do not know the difference between being honored and being feared and therefore do not understand the difference between biblical discipline and abuse. If spanking is legal where you live, and you use it as a form of discipline, please read the addendum at the end of this book.

Before you level any form of punishment on your Palm Tree, ask yourself:

- What was the intention of my child's heart?
- Have we talked about this before?
- Was the misbehavior intentional?
- Is my child tired or ill?

- When last did my child eat? What did he eat? (There is such a thing as a low- or high-blood-sugar tantrum!)
- Is my child simply immature or really disobedient?
- Is the behavior dangerous?
- Does my child know what she should have done instead?

Sometimes gentle instruction, healthy food, a nap, or similar attention to the root cause of the behavior is more appropriate than punishment.

3. Exhaustion and overcorrection: Exhaustion (sometimes called elimination) implies forced extension of a behavior until a child becomes exhausted of it. For example, a child who bites has to apologize and comfort the victim, then has to bite into a clean towel ten times for five seconds each time to "exhaust" the biting. It doesn't have the same satisfying effect for the biter to bite into the towel, and she realizes eventually that biting isn't as much fun as she thought it was. At the same time, if the biting was a fight-or-flight response to sensory overstimulation, the repeated biting will calm the child's physical frustration.

> *When we punish a child without insisting on the correct*
> *behavior, we haven't taught our child anything!*
> Ron Morrish, *Secrets of Discipline for Parents and Teachers*

If the victim is a sibling, it works well to have a planned ritual for caring for the victim. My Palm Tree, after biting his sister, had to rub ointment on the bite mark (which would be virtually invisible by that time), help put on a bandage, and rub her back for five minutes because she particularly liked back rubs. When the little guy resisted, we simply insisted firmly that everything be done. He soon decided it wasn't worth his while to bite, and he stopped doing it.

Exhaustion also works well with habits such as nail biting. For example, every time the little guy bites his nails, he has to wash his hand with soap, scrub his nails with a nail brush, and brush his teeth thoroughly to make sure all germs from his hands are killed.

Overcorrection is based on almost the same principle. It implies the repeated practice of the correct behavior every time incorrect behavior appears. Palm Trees' aversion to repetition makes this especially effective with them. Suppose your young child doesn't come when you call him. He will have to practice coming when called. He should listen to you calling him and quickly come running from ten different spots in the house. This stops being funny after the second or third exercise and leads to dramatically improved "hearing." Keep it up until you reach the tenth time, then say, "We're just practicing to make sure you come immediately next time I call you." The tween who slams a door could be required to close it softly four or five times to "learn to make it click rather than bang."

4. Immediate consequences: Palm Trees should not be made to feel like they are "awaiting trial." Take immediate action, unless you have a gawking audience of strangers who could make your Palm Tree mistake the situation for a stage. Bring the curtain down first! Don't wait until Dad comes home or until you can have a word with

your child's teacher. Also, immediately praise Palm Trees for exemplary behavior. The younger they are, the more important this is. Older kids can talk about yesterday's mischief and learn in retrospect.

5. Loss of or increase in social privileges: A Palm Tree is probably the only tree type for which time-out will yield desirable results. He won't think about his misbehavior, but he will experience a lack of attention and sympathy. Establish clear rules: he is not allowed to call from his time-out spot asking when time is up; he may not participate in any way in what others are doing. Create a time-out spot in a safe place away from all the action, excitement, and people. If a Palm Tree gets time-out on a chair in the front of a class, for example, it will only be a huge reward for him, because everyone's attention is focused on him and he has the entire stage to himself.

Palm Trees can be punished or rewarded effectively by being grounded or granted extra visiting privileges. The privilege of going to a friend's house or inviting friends over is a powerful incentive that will encourage Palm Trees to repeat the good behavior. Teenagers who don't respect curfews should be prevented from attending social events to "pay back" the stolen time.

Palm Trees are all about social response. My Palm Tree toddler once got very good advice from his sister for all the times he was sent to his room: "No, man, you are crying the wrong way. You must cry facing the door!"

6. Loss of or increase in material privileges: One of the most effective incentives for Palm Trees is a new toy, and the biggest deterrent is the loss of a favorite toy. Palm Trees' possessions are important to them even at a young age. Just think how proudly they want to show off their new toys at school! Cell phones, tablets, music players,

and handheld game consoles are the "toys" that can be taken away from teens and tweens.

Money is often important to Palm Trees—especially when they become teenagers—because it is synonymous with social potential. With money, Palm Trees can buy fun, popularity, fashion, social standing, and gifts for others. With little money, they can't follow the latest trends or spoil their friends. Consequently, they react well to increases or decreases in their allowances.

7. Visible rewards: Palm Trees are thrilled with a display of certificates, medals, and trophies. A weekly trophy placed in front of the table setting of the sibling with the best table manners can do wonders to motivate a Palm Tree preschooler.

A CULTIVATION PLAN FOR PALM TREES

The word *train* in Proverbs 22:6 has a rich meaning. It indicates that we are in for a long journey of instructing and motivating our kids. Here are suggestions for shaping our Palm Trees effectively:

1. We need to be serious about the behavior we want to teach our children, and willing to invest time and energy in the effort. We will not succeed without commitment.

2. We need to make sure our children truly know how to do the right thing. Do they really know how to make their beds, or are the beds still unmade because we haven't helped them with clear instructions and patient coaching?

3. We need to determine whether our children have become despondent because we didn't notice and reward the progress they have already made, even if it was only marginal. When we are

grounded in the principles of commitment, realism, and positive focus, we will be able to change their behavior much quicker and with fewer tears!

If we think all negative behavior can be "disciplined away," our parenting becomes very negative.

Another mistake we can make is trying to achieve too many goals at once. Palm Trees need to be "coached" in a focused way and with lots of praise if we want to see permanent results.

Whoever wants to reach a distant goal must take many small steps.

Helmut Schmidt

The following plan to change behavior can be used effectively with Palm Trees. Begin by making three lists in the following table of things you want to work on.

To Do Less	To Do More Often	Doing Great!

What does my Palm Tree do too often or incorrectly?

Write down things like: uses swear words, bites nails, hits sister, spits on other children, jumps on the furniture, sneaks cookies, uses up cell phone minutes within the first week of each month.

What does my Palm Tree do too infrequently or not at all?

Write down examples: doesn't pick up clothes from the floor, doesn't greet people by name, doesn't do chores around the house, doesn't eat vegetables, doesn't hand in school assignments on time.

What does my Palm Tree do right or often enough?

List things like: eagerly helps father in the garden, plays with the dog, comes immediately when called, goes to sleep without putting up a fight, has good manners. This third list is essential. Don't only nag about everything that is wrong; also focus on the good behavior, and give your child feedback or rewards every time he does the right thing.

Now rank each type of behavior according to how urgently you need to attend to it. Mark the highest priority with a 1, and so forth.

Choose only one thing from each list to start with.

Choose helpers. Grandma, a teacher, brothers, sisters, the baby-sitter, or your spouse can help by all expecting the same behavior (for instance, jumping on the trampoline instead of the furniture, and eating some veggies) from your child when they are in his presence. All can affirm his good manners.

Decide on a realistic time frame for each goal, and make sure it is a suitable time to work on this type of behavior. It may not be a good idea to try to teach your child saving skills during the December holidays. Examples: two weeks to learn to hang up the wet towels after bath time, or practicing for a month to get school assignments done on time.

Think about the behavior in the first column. Why does the Palm Tree do it? Ask, how can I take away the rewarding element? How can I ensure in a justified, meaningful way that the behavior will have negative consequences? Which behavior should replace it? How can I reward the desired behavior once my child starts behaving well?

For example, the fun he gets out of jumping on the furniture can be replaced by jumping on the trampoline. If he still chooses the sofa, he can't sit on the comfortable furniture during TV time; he gets a wooden chair instead. Choose rewards for the right behavior that will be highly motivational to your child's specific nature. For example, when he plays on the trampoline, take a snack out to add to the fun.

Take another example, a child who nags for an extra story before bedtime. If you usually give in, that's the reward. The nagging works. You'll have to be firm and not give in once during the two-week period or longer. We practice going to sleep peacefully after one story. If my Palm Tree nags about it, the following night's story will be taken away. If she goes to sleep peacefully, we will have story time the next night. If she can go to sleep without nagging for three nights in a row, there will be an extra story on night four. We count down the nights by putting up enormous glow-in-the-dark stars on the wall next to her bed. This way she will know how many nights of going to sleep peacefully are left before she earns an extra story. After the night with the extra story, we start counting from one again. There must be a realistic ceiling for the reward—a second story every fourth night.

Perhaps your teenager returns from social events long after curfew. It works because she doesn't mind you shouting at her afterward—she has already had her fun! The reward is that the punishment weighs much lighter than the fun. So you might decide that during the next month she will lose 10 percent of her allowance for every half hour she is late. However, if she sticks to the curfew, you'll increase her allowance by 20 percent. Connecting money to social events makes sense for a Palm Tree, especially in this context, because movies and pizza nights cost money.

Think about the behavior in the second list. Why doesn't your child do what you want him to do? Ask, does my Palm Tree really know what I expect and how to meet my demands? Is the behavior I expect realistic given my child's age and abilities? Should my child perhaps be trained more intensively before this behavior will work? How can I help my child rather than just evaluate how she is doing? Does she simply forget? If so, how can I help her remember? Patiently explain the new behavior that has to be acquired, practice it with your child, and give rewards until it becomes a habit. For example, involve him in preparing the veggies. Talk about the vitamins in different-colored foods. Have a "taste party" and try the veggies raw, steamed, and fried. Agree on a treat after dinner if he gets the desired portion of healthy food down tonight.

The child whose assignments are always late probably needs time-management skills, reminders on her phone or a calendar, and an incentive other than good grades.

Think about the behavior in the third list, and decide how you are going to reward it.

Hang a card on the back of your child's door with the heading "Caught Being Good," and write down spontaneous good behavior as soon as you notice it. Don't restrict what you notice to what you've written on the table above. It's very exciting for children to read a new positive comment every now and then, such as "Daddy noticed that you threw your banana peel in the trash without being asked!"

Jump in and follow through with your choices. Go through the lists often and make additions where necessary. Tick off the successes, and give yourself and your child a pat on the back for them. When you see a breakthrough in your child's behavior, you may take credit for it, because parenting is sometimes a thankless task.

DISCIPLE — SHAPING THE PALM TREE'S CHARACTER FOR GOD'S PURPOSE

The Palm Tree's most important journey is from superficiality and selfishness to deep and sincere love, because God often calls them to encourage, give abundantly, gather outsiders, and love all God's people passionately. They are often worshippers who bring praise to God in creative and generous ways.

Your efforts with the following character-shaping aspects will be crucial. As you do them practically, pray that God will do the work from the inside out through His Spirit. We can shape behavior, but He makes the springs of living water that will flow from your Palm Tree's heart.

Be patient and encouraging. These are the tough ones that take time. Fruit will come!

1. Choosing their friends with caution: Palm Trees are participants and joiners; therefore, of all the tree types, they are the most vulnerable to peer pressure. Some Palm Trees will do anything to promote their popularity. Our Palm Trees need to fine-tune their "friend detectors" and learn to look past appearances, because friends dressed in the latest fashion, those with the latest phone and funkiest hairstyles, are usually admired. We could expose them to older Palm Trees who have integrity so they could see that a person can be exciting and decent at the same time!

Become wise by walking with the wise; hang out
with fools and watch your life fall to pieces.
Proverbs 13:20

2. Admitting mistakes and telling the truth: Palm Trees seem to be born with a law degree and can raise convincing arguments about everything. They use this ability to defer blame and to create reasonable doubt. We should regard this in a very serious light, because this is one of the big character flaws of the "unpruned" Palm Tree. Their honesty is crucial to their calling. It is all right to use exaggeration to entertain, but they need to know where the truth, the whole truth, and nothing but the truth is an integrity issue. They are often the evangelists, and their most important message won't be believed if the other words they say are half-truths.

The issue is how to know when they are lying, isn't it? FBI profiler and interrogation expert Jack Trimarco names four signs that show that your child is most likely lying:[8]

- Double is trouble: A lying child may repeat your statements in a ploy to gain time to think up a believable response.
- Facing the facts: Changing facial expressions, or gestures such as nose scratching or brow wiping, often signal dissembling.
- Missing a beat: Since kids know it's wrong to fib, they may deliver the whopper in a lowered voice, or change the tone or tempo of their speech.

- Talking too much: A less-than-truthful child may
  feel compelled to fill empty airtime with unsolic-
  ited information. Unless your kid is the type who
  reports every detail, rambling is a sure sign he's
  feeding you baloney.

3. Avoiding impulsive words and actions: Palm Trees often feel
remorse, though it usually comes much too late for the parents' liking!
Why do our children make these mistakes? Why don't they think?
They know what is right, but still they don't do it! These are a few of
the common complaints of Palm Trees' parents. If we plan to help
them attain responsible adulthood, we will have to ensure that our
Palm Trees understand from a young age the consequences of irresponsible choices, especially of those impulsive actions that hurt others.

4. To listen to others: Palm Trees would rather speak than listen.
If they never learn to give others the same opportunity, Palm Trees
come across as being self-centered. To teach this principle of good
listening, use an object at the dinner table, such as a salt shaker or
serving spoon. The one holding it may speak, while all the others listen with their whole bodies: hold arms and legs still, face the speaker,
and look him or her in the eyes. Once Palm Trees understand how
gifted they are in the "people business," they will want to listen more!

5. To be loyal: Palm Trees are sometimes fair-weather friends.
They don't mean to be nasty. They simply can't see why they should
keep on playing with someone who doesn't buy them candy during
break times or who doesn't think up exciting games anymore. Palm
Trees also have difficulty staying loyal to a team that loses or a school
that seems boring. Infidelity has destroyed countless Palm Tree men

and women of God. But they can learn to be in a relationship for what they can give to it, not for what they can get. Teaching loyalty, by expecting them to remain on a losing team until the end of the season or to visit a friend who is too sick to play fun games, for example, is a great starting point to prevent this from happening to your Palm Tree in adulthood.

LET'S GET PRACTICAL

Because a positive approach is essential with Palm Trees, here are a couple of exercises to help you identify what that approach looks like. For each statement made below, indicate which kind of statement it is, then "translate" it into a friendly, positive alternative:

Kinds of statements:

A: Accusations

P: Personal attacks

C: Criticism

N: Negative instructions

T: Threats

____ "If you are not in the bathroom in five seconds, you are sure to get a spanking!"

____ "What is wrong with you? By this time, one would think you would remember to flush the toilet!"

____ "Look at this mess! You have once again not cleaned up your room."

____ "Don't pick your nose. You won't find any diamonds there."

____ "As usual, you're late for school. You're too slow to catch a snail."

___ "You are not allowed to sit on my couch when your feet are dirty."

___ "If you only listened when I warned you, Grandma's expensive vase wouldn't be broken now!"

___ "This crying is nonsense. Stop it now, before I give you a reason to cry."

It's usually very simple to recast negative instructions in a positive way. Look at the examples of common instructions below, and then replace the rest. (Once you get into the habit of starting your instructions with something other than "Don't," it will have a huge impact on your parenting style!)

"Don't eat with your mouth open."
IMPROVEMENT: "Please close your mouth while you're chewing."

"Don't splash water all over the bathroom floor."
IMPROVEMENT: "Keep the bathroom floor dry, please."

"Don't drag your backpack."
IMPROVEMENT: "_____."

"Don't pick your nose."
IMPROVEMENT: "_____."

"Don't disobey me!"
IMPROVEMENT: "_____."

CHAPTER 5

PARENTING THE ROSE BUSH

Read this chapter if your child tested Rose Bush, Box-Rose, Palm-Rose, Pine-Rose, or Contra-Pine. These trees are all in the Rose Bush family. Also read chapter 9 if your child is not a "pure" Rose Bush.

In this chapter:

- Meet Kevin, a natural Rose Bush.
- Develop—how to nurture the nature of a young Rose Bush.
- Direct—what and how to teach a Rose Bush.
- Dialogue—how to speak the Rose Bush dialect.
- Discipline—how to train the Rose Bush way.
- Disciple—shaping the Rose Bush's character for God's purpose.

When looking for a tree type to represent this temperament, I searched for a tree that was strong in nature—prickly but productive. A prickly pear cactus initially came to mind, probably because people with this temperament can be aggressive, hot tempered, or insensitive. There are, however, so many wonderful, positive traits in people with this nature who have been "pruned" correctly. Roses are such exceptional flowers that they provided a better analogy for the extraordinary productivity and potential of this temperament type.

Rose bushes require aggressive pruning, but they're tough. Without attention they'll survive, but they'll produce more thorns and fewer flowers. Even if you don't breathe down their necks, Rose Bushes will drive themselves to do their work.

The possibility of fame and success is a special package given to Rose Bush babies at birth. Rose Bushes have the ability to rise above the rest thanks to their strong drive and competitiveness, which is simply ingrained in their nature. Unfortunately, roses also have thorns (except when the thorns are deliberately bred out of them), which makes them challenging saplings to shape. They should not be tackled with bare hands.

MEET KEVIN, THE NATURAL ROSE BUSH

Roses are red, and they tend to draw blood … especially in the early years!

When Kevin was only a year old, his mother had to keep a constant eye on the rearview mirror because the little rascal could unbuckle his car-seat restraint. Many months before the dreaded second birthday, Kevin threw unreserved tantrums at the sight of a hairbrush, a toothbrush, a clean diaper, shampoo, vegetables, a closed door, or another child near one of his toys. It was easier to straighten a banana than to strap him into his car seat.

By the time Kevin was three (going on ten), he all but forbade his parents from touching him. He dressed himself, brushed his own teeth, applied his own sunscreen, locked and unlocked all doors, and—to the frustration of his control-freak mother—made his own sandwiches. When he turned four, Kevin acted up in a restaurant by throwing his knife and fork to the floor because they didn't have pictures of his favorite cartoon characters on them.

To get through Kevin's childhood with their mental health intact, his parents followed the general strategy of picking their battles. They averted conflict by giving in, begging, and leaving as many decisions as possible up to him.

Unfortunately, Kevin turned into a little tyrant, and fewer and fewer people came to visit. He was too bossy for some of the other kids' liking, and he played with such vigor that he hurt a few of his friends. Three sets of parents told his parents they would never visit with their children again.

When his younger brother, Josh, was born, Kevin stepped into the parenting role and directed his brother's life. Kevin told Josh how many forkfuls of beans he had to eat before he could leave the table. When Kevin felt Josh was moving or processing too slowly, he spurred Josh on in a strict teacher voice. Kevin competed to win in everything without making allowance for his brother's smaller size or undeveloped skills. Who could throw the ball farther and kick it higher? Always Kevin!

It was clear that Kevin thought, *The world will be a much better place if everyone would just accept, once and for all, that I am the boss. I will not stop until everyone agrees to this state of affairs. I think we're almost there—just one or two more loooong screams ... just a few louder protests. I have my dad in my pocket and, of course, Grandpa and Grandma too. I am still working on Mom, though. She's tough, like me!*

As Kevin grows, his parents will find that he can be like a hand grenade from which the pin has already been pulled—especially during his teen years. But they'll also be amazed by everything Kevin can accomplish on his own. He will probably excel as a leader and actively participate in debates and other student affairs. He will go after all that life has to offer. He may clash with the people around him because he wants to be in control of everything and everyone, but he will think big and realize his own dreams. His persistence will make him a winner.

People will likely say many of these things about Kevin someday:

- "You are a control freak."
- "You don't take no for an answer."
- "You are a self-starter, a go-getter."
- "If you can't do it, no one can."
- "You don't beat about the bush, do you?"
- "Do you ever take a break?"

DEVELOP — HOW TO NURTURE THE NATURE OF A YOUNG ROSE BUSH

In your child's Tall Trees Kids Profile Report, these tailor-made needs will be among those listed as the Rose Bush's "Fertilizer."

1. Lots of playtime and exercise: Like Palm Trees, Rose Bushes have lots of energy. They simply shouldn't be inactive and cooped up

indoors. If they don't get rid of the heaps of energy, they'll convert it into aggression. An exhausted Rose Bush toddler is less likely to fight you at bath time. When we discovered that little trick, we scheduled "aerobics classes" at five in the afternoon.

Rose Bushes don't want to just run and climb—they want to be able to scream loudly, throw things, kick, hit, tug, and push. If we don't facilitate appropriate forms of these activities for them, they'll get creative in troubling ways. Rose Bush teenagers who don't participate in sports or exercise are, without exception, negative and moody. They feel exhilarated if they can push themselves to the limit. Encourage them to participate in sports or at least to go out on their skateboards or mountain bikes or to take a walk.

2. Chances to practice new skills: We tend to overprotect Rose Bushes because their daring nature makes us anxious. They always want to go faster, higher, and farther. Consequently, we make the mistake of standing between them and their stunts. We should rather choose safe places and suitable times for them to test their abilities. Get into the swimming pool with your two-year-old to save him from drowning when he tries to prove that he can swim. Don't simply refuse because you know he can't swim. He needs the opportunity to try. Enroll him in swim lessons.

3. A set of fixed boundaries: Rose Bushes would much rather set their own boundaries than accept ours and will constantly try to shift those boundaries. Make the boundaries that you decide are important very clear! Boundaries help Rose Bushes with self-control because they define which areas of control belong to them and which areas belong to the parents. They can rule their country when they have the map of the borders.

4. Regular and consistent correction: Some parents tend to avoid confrontation with Rose Bushes because it can get so explosive, but we won't be doing anyone a favor if we overlook things that are indeed unacceptable. The sooner we start, the sooner we will be finished with the intensely confrontational part of their discipline! Parents who say they've raised a Rose Bush without things ever getting a little ugly are parents who have likely been trained by their Rose Bush children to play the game their way. Rose Bushes, more than any other tree type, must learn to face the consequences of their choices every time. They will likely continue challenging their parents if they get away with a serious offense even once.

5. Reasons for instructions and punishment: Rose Bushes are goal oriented, rational, and logical. They want to understand (they *need* to understand) why they are expected to do something before they are willing to cooperate. If they can see reason, they gladly do what is needed, but it's very hard for them to obey just because we told them to.

When your Rose Bush shows her thorns, it may help to ask, "Do you know why I want you to do it?"[9] What seems logical to you might not necessarily be obvious to her! Once Rose Bushes understand your point of view, they may suggest a different way of accomplishing your objective. Allow for this, as long as the outcome is the same.

6. Praise for good decisions and choices: Rose Bushes are naturally good at decision making, problem solving, and choosing. Encourage these talents by letting your Rose Bush solve problems, then providing feedback on how she did. Be specific: "You decided to put on your jacket this morning, even if you don't always like wearing it. It was a

smart idea, because it was a cold day. You made a good decision." Or after controlling her anger over not being given permission to go on a high school camping trip: "You chose not to manipulate me for a yes. That was wise, because I am more likely to say yes to a person who understands the difference between rights and privileges."

7. An example of fair and respectful leadership: Rose Bushes will be leaders. Some will be good ones, others bad ones, but one thing is certain—they will lead. It's in their nature. Someone will always follow them. Unfortunately, many Rose Bush leaders are harsh. We should therefore expose our young Rose Bushes to strong but sensitive people so we can teach them that one can be a "boss" without being a villain! The best example, of course, should be our own.

8. Opportunities to lead and control: Allow them to be in charge of appropriate responsibilities from an early age. This preparation for future leadership is important, even if you present it as a game. If one has a house full of children (three or more), the Rose Bush can get a chance to be sheriff. Everyone with complaints takes their problems or requests to the sheriff first, and only when he is stumped may Mom and Dad's help be called in. This gives him good practice in problem solving and handling conflicts.

The most important aim of Rose Bushes is to be in control. Their second most important aim is to be more grown up than they really are. This is the reason why we frequently lock horns with them. But you can support their budding maturity. For example, put your Rose Bush in charge of the remote control for the DVD player. Make her responsible for answering the phone when you can't. Allow her to check the clock for dinnertime, call siblings when the food is ready, turn the stove burners on or off (under your supervision, of course!), blow out the candles after dinner, and switch on the dishwasher.

9. Responsibilities: The other tree types might not enjoy chores as much, but Rose Bushes feel a sense of self-worth, pride, and maturity when they have responsibilities. Each chore becomes an opportunity for them to prove themselves. Therefore, they should be given chores in and around the house from an early age.

Here is a starter list of appropriate chores:

- Feed the pets.
- Bathe the pets.
- Walk the dog.
- Wash, dry, or put away the dishes.
- Set or clear the table.
- Make the bed.
- Get up on time by using an alarm clock.
- Help with food preparations.
- Prepare breakfast cereal.
- Get dressed without help.
- Help a younger sibling with a task.
- Help unpack and put away groceries.
- Wash or sweep the floors.
- Wash the windows.
- Vacuum the carpet.
- Put cups and saucers on a tray when guests are visiting.
- Make sandwiches for school.
- Sort DVDs and Blu-rays.

- Tidy a bookcase.
- Clean the car.
- Put away bath toys.
- Clean the bath.
- Put clothes in the laundry hamper.
- Pack away toys.
- Put on shoes without help.
- Make tea and coffee.
- Fill up sugar bowls or salt and pepper shakers.
- Monitor the swimming-pool pump.
- Rake leaves and weed flower beds.
- Get mail from the mailbox.

10. To be challenged physically, intellectually, and socially: Rose Bushes have to run races, be quizzed, compete with older children, and be tested in several other ways. The young ones may become destructive or aggressive (breaking toys or playing rough), and the older kids tend to become oppositional unless they have the chance to give their best every now and then.

Let them set a record for getting dressed or cleaning up the fastest, mowing the lawn, setting the table, or being the first to try a new exotic dish from mom. Keep charts and take pictures. Reward them when they break a previous best. A social challenge can be something like, "Your cousins are coming to visit today. Let's see if you can play in such a way that none of them complains that you were mean."

11. To make choices: Choices are synonymous with control, responsibility, and decision making. Rose Bushes hate feeling they don't have a choice. This makes them unnecessarily rebellious.

Sometimes we simply have to rephrase our instructions so that the Rose Bushes think that they are exercising their own free will, because this will diminish the conflict considerably. All children feel more capable when given the opportunity to make real decisions.

When four-and-a-half-year-old Rose Bush Katelyn refused to pick up her toys, her mom stated her expectations as a choice: "Katelyn, you can either have a bath first and then pick up your toys, or pick up your toys and then take a bath. Which one would you like to do first?" This proud moment of remembering that a Rose Bush child needs more choices went up in flames when Katelyn answered, "No! I don't want any of those choices. I want to play outside!" Mom, taken aback by this, turned around to see her Palm Tree teenager laughing hysterically at her failed attempt because "it soooo backfired!"

Disobedience, however, is never an option! Mom might have said, "I'm sorry you don't like those choices, but that's what's available right now. Do you want to decide, or should I?" At bedtime you can say, "It's time to go to bed. You can choose which story you would like to hear." When the battle about clothes looms on the horizon, you might say, "You need to wear a jacket. Which one do you pick?"

12. To prove themselves reliable: Freedom and space for trial and error are important to Rose Bushes because they can measure how grown up they are against these. When they realize we trust them with more time, money, and choices as they prove to be reliable, they often amaze us with behavior that is surprising for their age.

If you have a Rose Bush, I strongly recommend putting this note on the fridge:

Give your Rose Bush a chance today to
make a choice
make a decision
solve a problem
give an opinion
lead someone
complete a task independently
prove his [or her] reliability and
take on a challenge.

DIRECT — WHAT AND HOW TO TEACH A ROSE BUSH

It should be clear by now that Rose Bushes don't like us to hold their hands the whole time! The most successful approach with them works almost like a yo-yo—we say what we want quickly, then release the little ones to try without our supervision. If it doesn't work out so well, we tug gently at the string so we can explain again, then we let go again … every time a bit more.

Our Rose Bushes need to learn:

1. To accept no as an answer and not to manipulate: Parents of Rose Bushes know only too well how this little word can open the floodgates of fury. Rose Bushes hate being denied their wishes. It has the same effect on them that a red flag has on a bull. They pull out all the stops: scream, fall down, kick, hit, bite, insult, threaten, or throw things. This type of behavior is their style of manipulation.

Explain in simple terms to your child what the word *manipulation* means. Under no circumstances should you give in to manipulative behavior, even if the behavior is no more than a moaning voice, droopy shoulders, and a sigh or eye rolling. Even these subtler manipulation techniques should be pointed out, rejected, and stopped by ensuring that they never succeed.

Always explain to your child an effective alternative behavior. For example, you could say, "If you talk to me in your friendly voice, I will listen, but if you are rude, the answer will automatically be no."

2. To differentiate between their domain and that of their parents: Rose Bushes need to wield their scepter somewhere, but parents have the mandate to decide where their kingdom starts and ends. We can use the power struggle for control at the dinner table as an example. Dr. James Dobson warns that parents should choose the fights at the dinner table carefully because we don't often win them.[10]

Imagine a Rose Bush popping into the kitchen before dinner and announcing, "This is not nice food. I hate beans, and I hate that brown sauce with the chicken." In response to this we should say firmly, "I decide what food to prepare. I choose food that will help you grow. That is my job. You eat healthy food so I know when I can give you snacks that are less healthy. That's your job."

Another example would be, "I have to see to it that you are dressed warmly so that you don't catch a cold. That is why I am making you wear a jacket. That is my job. I am going to do my job because I want to be a good mommy. You have five jackets to choose from. That is your job."

3. To lose with dignity and win with modesty: This is a difficult one! Rose Bushes have thrown many a board game to the floor the moment they aren't leading anymore, or assaulted a teammate for making a mistake on the sports field. They can keep on defending themselves insistently, claiming it was unfair that they lost and that the

game didn't really count. Of course, when they win, they can be just as insistent in rubbing salt in the wounds of the losers. Have a chat beforehand about good sportsmanship. "Can you remember what you like to do when you win? You stick out your tongue at the loser. What can you do to show your happiness without making the loser feel bad?" or "Today you are going to be in a race with that fast boy again. Last week you tripped him as he wanted to pull ahead of you, and you screamed. What will you do today if someone outruns you?"

Expose your Rose Bushes to frequent competition, and sometimes manipulate the outcome by pitting them against stronger competitors so they don't win every time.

4. To be a team player and cooperate under someone else's leadership: This is one of the most difficult challenges Rose Bushes will have—it is not in their nature to be followers. I believe the best place to learn this is in the family environment. Mom and Dad are the leaders who need to be followed, and siblings are the team members. Strong foundations are built by expecting Rose Bushes to treat parents with respect and obedience, and siblings with love and fairness.

Rose Bushes may need to be supervised in social situations and stopped when they become too domineering. We can't allow them to develop a circle of willing subjects who will grant their every wish. A relative once told me that their Rose Bush daughter never walked at the preschool. She had "servants" who carried her between the gate and the classroom and to the playground and back. The princess did not take her dethroning lying down (except for the part where she threw a tantrum on the school grounds).

5. To appreciate privileges: Rose Bushes can act like royalty, as seen in the example above—expecting respect, service, loyalty, subservience,

obedience, compliance, and cooperation from everyone around them. They tend to take for granted that their laundry is washed and put back in their closets or their food lands on their plates three times a day according to their tastes. If parents tolerate this attitude in young Rose Bushes, it develops into full-blown entitlement when they are adults. We do their future spouses and social circles a favor when we constantly cultivate appreciation in them.

One of the best antidotes for becoming spoiled is exposure to underprivileged children. It is easy to arrange this. Call your church office and ask for the phone number of your social worker or the leaders of a charity project. Ask how you and your children, and even some friends and their parents, can get involved.

6. To express emotion appropriately: Empower your Rose Bushes by nurturing their emotional intelligence. Explain to them what emotions are—feelings inside that we can release or "let out" in different ways. We can release them in right or wrong ways with facial expressions, actions, and words. Other people get hurt when we vent emotions in the wrong way. We feel better, however, and we're less likely to hurt people's feelings when we emote in the right way.

We can also use our emotions constructively. Emotions are like battery power. They can urge us on. They can also be like wild horses, but once we harness them correctly, they can take us all the way to our goals!

Emotional intelligence can help prevent tantrums when possible. The idea is to help our Rose Bushes avoid getting angry of their own accord so they can learn self-control strategies. When they realize that they do not have to react in anger, they experience a feeling of control over their emotions—something that will improve their self-image.

7. To relieve aggression in acceptable ways: The thorns of a Rose Bush are sharp, and we often get pricked by them. They can have such vicious explosions that we feel we need to punish them. But often punishment only makes matters worse. Each tantrum is, however, an opportunity to improve a Rose Bush's self-control.

Before we can address anger management, we have to realize that many tantrums can be prevented if we understand what triggers our specific child. For example, when we give our child who often has a meltdown in the mall something to eat in the car before a shopping trip, his blood-sugar levels will be normal when we walk past the candy shelf. With a child who easily becomes overwhelmed, we may need to go home as soon as we see the first sign that the toddler is becoming overstimulated by all the friends and noisy play at the park. If you have a child with sensory-processing challenges, let her put on comfortable clothes before you undertake a long journey by car.

Deal with every temper tantrum, even though it would be so much easier to ignore them. I do not subscribe to the notion that ignored misbehavior will magically dissipate. Children need learned skills and do-overs to replace inappropriate habits. First acknowledge and validate the anger ("I see you are frustrated because your sister has all the toys"), and then deal with the behavior, because a Rose Bush will stop his unacceptable behavior quicker if he can see that you understand his feelings.

Then tell him exactly which part of the behavior is unacceptable. "But you know you are not allowed to bite" or "You are not allowed to slam doors."

If the situation is totally out of control and the child is incapable of listening to you or stopping his behavior at this point, physically intervene and remove the child from the situation. Of course, this applies only to children under the age of ten. Older children should be able to step away of their own accord and cool down without our physical involvement. Once everyone has calmed down, you can talk about it. Your child should first apologize to whomever was affected by his outburst. End the conversation with a constructive plan for similar situations in the future.

Prepare your child when an explosive situation is imminent. When you realize that your child is about to face a situation in which he would usually explode, warn him so that he has a chance to prepare himself mentally and show you, and himself, that he doesn't have to lose control.

If a child is continuously aggressive, attempt to find out why. Aggression is often a Rose Bush's reaction to a situation that makes her feel out of control or the reaction to someone's aggression toward her. For example, if a child who is brought up too strictly is not allowed to make any choices or to make any decisions, she will undoubtedly be aggressive. Sometimes this is her clumsy way of dealing with unfulfilled needs.

All too often, aggression stems from a fight-or-flight response rooted in sensory-processing issues. Our child has become over-stimulated by other kids, tight clothing, difficult tasks, heat—even processed food!—and has had meltdowns of the Rose Bush variety! An assessment by an occupational therapist is the best starting point. Therapy and techniques you can use at home to help your child manage sensory overload can go a long way to lessen outbursts.

The best way to get rid of aggression is to spend it before the child becomes out of control. There are many games and quick, simple actions to help a little Rose Bush with this. Turn these ideas into a competition, or dare her to do it the loudest, fastest, highest, or longest she can:

- Let her throw something unbreakable, like a ball of clay, to the ground hard and repeatedly.
- Let her hit something, like a punching bag, a pillow, or a beanbag.
- Give her a blunt pencil and allow her to poke holes in a cardboard box, egg carton, or polystyrene container.
- Let her tear up a newspaper or crumple it up and throw it at a basket.
- Choose something in the backyard that she may kick—for example, old car tires, cardboard boxes, or a bag full of grass or leaves.
- Wrestle with your Rose Bush, or race her.
- See who can yell the loudest.
- Let her stomp her feet, jump up and down, and swing her arms.
- Let her smash weeds with a stick.
- Use calming techniques such as therapeutic sensory brushing (consult an occupational therapist for instruction), hugging, and other "deep pressure" soothing tricks.

A man who does not know how to be angry
does not know how to be good.
Henry Ward Beecher

Our own aggression has a huge impact on our children. They initially learn ways of dealing with emotions from us. Many Rose Bush parents complain about their children's outbursts but excuse their own explosions by calling them the result of "a short fuse" or "stress."

Anger must be confessed as sin if it has hurt other people. We want our children to take ownership of their emotions, and we have to set an example in this by apologizing to the Lord and our family when we have had an outburst: "I am sorry that I have just exploded at the table. Please forgive me. I should have gone to my room to cool off. It is not your fault that I am angry."

Don't keep your anger behind closed doors. My mother-in-law referred to it as "bedroom boardroom"—that intense, hushed conversation between parents late at night in their room when they think the children are asleep. We can teach our children a lot about anger management if we resolve some of our differences in front of them without outbursts or physical violence.

We would be wise to identify our own triggers and have a plan in place to deal with our emotions in a better way, preferably by being accountable to someone who can monitor whether we are handling our anger constructively.[11]

> *When children push your buttons, you react from your*
> *reptilian brain, and reptiles eat their young!*
> Dr. Jane Nelsen, *Positive Time-Out*

Make it a house rule that nobody needs to listen to shouting. When someone gets hysterical or insulting, the other person may walk away. The table and car are fight-free zones for the sake of digestion and road safety.

If it seems like the aggression gets worse or doesn't improve at all, even if you make an effort to handle it as suggested above, call in the help of a professional. I believe play therapists can be the best choice when a young child needs help with aggression. They are qualified to accompany you as parents, and your child, through this phase.

Our Rose Bushes learn best:

- by making their own choices and dealing with the consequences
- when they are challenged to find their own solutions
- by doing something on their own by means of trial and error
- when the focus is on the positive
- when there is a clear aim with which they can identify
- when they are treated as valuable people, worthy in their own right
- when parents give them space and don't constantly breathe down their necks
- when directives are short, powerful, and practical
- when they can see a challenge and reward in a task
- when the parent expresses confidence in their abilities and success
- from a role model whom they respect

DIALOGUE — HOW TO SPEAK THE ROSE BUSH DIALECT

How does God speak to Rose Bushes?

When the Lord reveals Himself to Rose Bushes, He shows them His glorious strength and the magnificence of His being. The apostle Paul was an obvious Rose Bush. With Paul, it was necessary to bring him to a complete standstill and strike him with blindness because nothing less would have made him abandon his obstinate mission to kill Christians (Acts 9:1–9).

Rose Bushes are given difficult assignments that might overwhelm the other tree types because Rose Bushes often influence many other people through their actions (Acts 9:15–16).

The Lord scolds and confronts them when necessary (Acts 9:4–5).

The Lord encourages them and reassures them that He will give them strength (Acts 18:9).

He gives them challenges and doesn't shy away from telling them how difficult the tasks will be (Acts 9:15).

How should we talk to our Rose Bushes?

> *It is always a great mistake to command when*
> *you are not sure you will be obeyed.*
> Honoré Gabriel de Riqueti, comte de Mirabeau, *Memoires of Mirabeau*

Keep the following principles in mind to ensure your Rose Bush hears you:

Be sure of yourself—they are looking for a sign of doubt in your words! The typical advice that we should stoop to the child's level when

Customer Name: Jones, Elba Judith

Items that you checked out

Title
Growing kids with character : nurturing
your child 's potential, purpose, and
passion
ID: 31815117897342
Due: Monday, August 20, 2018

Total items: 1
Account balance: $3.75
7/30/2018 3:38 PM
Checked out: 1
Overdue: 0
Hold requests: 0
Ready for pickup: 0

Don't miss the fun! MidPointe's Summer
Reading Program -- June 1 - July 31

we talk does not apply to a Rose Bush unless you want to have a bit of quality time. In discipline, you would be wise not to do it. They may have been waiting for the moment and an opportunity to put their teeth in your jugular. I exaggerate, but I've seen the look in many Rose Bushes' eyes: "If my mom keeps up with that voice and that face, I'm going to lose it. I'm going to eat her alive!"

Remember to add one good reason for the instructions you give. Rose Bushes don't obey an instruction because you say so, but because it makes sense to them. When she asks "Why?" questions in turn, don't take them as an assault on your authority. Give her the benefit of the doubt. She's probably looking for a reason to cooperate with you.

If the Rose Bush doesn't listen and you feel like screaming, go to her, take her face in your hands (unless she dislikes this sort of touch), and say softly but firmly what you expect. Moving closer says "Yes, I'm talking to you" much more eloquently than an increase of ten decibels.

If you are very angry, say so to prevent your Rose Bush from unwittingly setting off a land mine. Instead of shouting, say something like, "My blood is boiling," or use a gesture, such as pointing to the wet towel on the floor and frowning.

Be direct, unequivocal, and brief. This means that you shouldn't ask for cooperation, but rather insist on it calmly and kindly. Long-winded instructions irritate Rose Bushes. They turn each point into a negotiation.

Keep it impersonal and unemotional. This is especially important when your Rose Bush is being rude.

Kind words can be short and easy to speak, but their echoes are truly endless.
Mother Teresa

Try, as much as possible, to use positive words when giving your instructions: "Let's see if you can put away all those blocks in the right place without help. I will time how quickly you can do it." This works a lot better than threats, such as, "I am coming back in five minutes, and you'll be sorry if I find one block out of place!"

When your child starts understanding more reason—at about six years of age—you can start exchanging many directives with conversations. Before announcing a rigid rule ("Your bike has to be locked to the pipe outside the kitchen every afternoon by five o'clock or you'll lose your bike-riding privileges"), show your Rose Bush that you respect his abilities by taking his perspective into account. State the problem: "Two bikes have already been stolen from the front yard this year. We cannot afford a repeat of that." Ask him to suggest a solution: "How can you make sure that it never happens again?" Give him a chance to suggest a few ideas. Ask questions if the solutions are not satisfactory: "How will you remember that every day? What time do you think will be best for this? Which privileges do you think it would be fair to lose if you don't look after your bike in this way? What will we do if it doesn't work and your bike is stolen?"

Also make a positive assumption that your child will be obedient by using the word *when* instead of *if*. For example, "When your homework is finished, you may go and watch that movie you've been dying to see." Don't attack or confront your child if you can help it because this provokes arguments and excuses and doesn't encourage obedience. For more on this, see "Let's Get Practical" at the end of this chapter.

In summary:

- Give clear instructions.
- Give reasons.
- Give consequences.
- Get out of the way until it is done.
- Give recognition for success.

How can we listen to our Rose Bushes better?

Allow your older Rose Bush a fair chance to state her case. You may make a strict rule that she has to speak in a friendly manner without accusations or insults.

Make sure you understand her correctly by repeating the words you have heard. For example, "It sounds to me as if you're saying we were stricter with you about your bedtime than we are with your sister, and you feel it is unfair. You want us to make up for this by being stricter with your sister and more lenient with you. Is that what you are saying?" After this, you can accept her suggestions or explain why you won't.

Listen for indications that they are ready for more responsibility. "I hate it when you tell me to go to bed" could mean "I think I am old enough to go to bed at eight without being told."

A Rose Bush can come across as being blunt and tactless, and you are welcome to correct this. If you take each remark personally, those thorns are going to draw more blood than is necessary. She most likely doesn't mean to be as rude as she sounds.

Listen carefully, because Rose Bushes hope you won't see through their manipulation tactics. Look out for their ability to play on your feelings of guilt.

Even when their request is completely unreasonable, you could respond in many ways besides just saying no and triggering them in the process:

- "That is an idea. Let me think about it. When do you need a final answer?" (They are more likely to accept a no that comes after some thought.)
- "What is your plan?" (They may come up with the same restrictions you would have given!)
- "Is it in accordance with our house rules?" (The objective rule is less confrontational than your no.)
- "How can you be certain that it can work?" (This is your opportunity to gauge your child's insight.)
- "Why should I say yes this time when I said no in the past?" (This gives them a chance to share what they have learned over time.)

DISCIPLINE — HOW TO TRAIN THE ROSE BUSH WAY

Each tree type has its own pruning and watering needs. These approaches work the best with Rose Bushes:

1. Loss of or increase in physical freedom. Rose Bushes hate feeling cooped up, and they blossom when they have freedom and options. We can use this effectively in their discipline. Rose Bushes who lose control completely can literally be held, or at least placed in a confined space, until they have calmed down. With the very little ones, you can simply hold the disobedient hand, foot, or arm for a

few moments while explaining that you will have to control it until they are able to control it themselves.

Rose Bushes who, for example, don't come when they are called can be required to hold their mom's hand everywhere they go. If they listen and obey, however, they may walk alone—a big reward of freedom! With the school-age Rose Bush, use a phrase like, "You must be home within thirty minutes after school to have a snack and start with your homework. You can get home in time by yourself, or I can pick you up at the gate every day like I did last year." This is a way of saying, "If you want more freedom, you have to earn it and use it wisely."

If your Rose Bushes behave the way you expect them to, reward them with more physical freedom. This means, for example, that they may go somewhere alone, provided it is safe, that they may stay out later, or that they may walk through a store on their own and meet at the checkout later.

2. Raised or lowered status: Rose Bushes want to feel grown up and important and to be treated that way. Their status inside and outside the house is important to them. Their position in the family and their correlating rights—for example, bedtimes and the amount of allowance they receive—are equally important. Rose Bushes see being allowed to stay up later as a higher status, and this is usually a worthwhile reward for them. Use status as an incentive in this way: "When you have learned not to throw a tantrum when it is time to stop watching television, we will put you in charge of the remote control for the TV." This is, of course, the second-highest position in some households, next to being the keeper of the Wi-Fi password!

3. Loss of or increase in choices: When we clash with our Rose Bushes, it's usually because they don't like our decisions and would

prefer to make their own choices. We can effectively motivate them by increasing their choices when they show the capacity to be responsible for more.

When Rose Bushes try to enforce their wills in unacceptable ways (such as manipulation), their choices should be decreased: "If you can't get into the car without fussing, I will decide where you sit, and I will fasten your seat belt." "If you lie on the floor when you have to get dressed, you will have to wear the clothes I pick."

4. A spanking (where legal and in line with your convictions; see the addendum at the end of this book): I can already hear the protest from Rose Bushes' parents: "We tried spanking—it doesn't work!" This only means the Rose Bush won the bluffing game. I'm prepared to bet that your Rose Bush gave you at least one of the following reactions to a spanking in an attempt to dissuade you from ever using it as a means of discipline again:

- Your Rose Bush hit you back.
- Your Rose Bush shouted, "That didn't hurt!" as a way to hide the shame of crying.
- Your Rose Bush made an insulting remark such as, "I hate you!"
- Your Rose Bush wreaked havoc in the place where you gave him the spanking. (This means you and he need to do hard work in the area of cultivating emotional intelligence and dealing with aggression.)
- Your Rose Bush turned red in the face but refused to cry, or she even smiled! This is just another example of defiance.

- Your Rose Bush evaded you so effectively that you decided the spanking was going to end up like something from a WWE wrestling match, and you didn't feel up to that, so you surrendered.
- Instead of improving after the spanking, your Rose Bush's behavior got worse.
- Your Rose Bush moved the behavior to another location (like Grandma's house, the church, the shopping center, the entrance to the nursery school, or the backseat of the car), where you weren't present and/or wouldn't administer a spanking.

Never get into the ring with your Rose Bush. If he uses the behavior described above to challenge you, don't take the bait! These behaviors are all rooted in your Rose Bush child's determination to win. The aggression is not caused by the spanking as such, but by the fact that Rose Bushes feel a need to get even. To their minds, you scored a point. They want to go for the best out of three, then the best out of five, and so on. Consider acknowledging this: "You acting this way after a spanking tells me you think this is a fight that I am trying to win. You want to fight back. It is not a fight. It is me helping you learn that wrong choices lead to pain. You disobeyed. I punished you. It is over."

If the behavior for which the child was punished in the first place is followed by more bad behavior, restrain yourself and say calmly, "It's a shame that you have done something else that deserves another punishment. That was a bad choice. You know I cannot allow you to do that." Then give a second consequence.

We can cry about our children for a short while or
for a long time—it all depends on our willingness to
discipline them properly when they are still young!

Author unknown

5. Logical consequences: Because Rose Bushes are logical and rational, it confuses them when we give arbitrary or random punishments and rewards. If you announce they can't watch television when they forget to put their clothes in the laundry basket, they'll feel unfairly treated. Be careful to choose the punishments and rewards sensibly, and make expectations and consequences clear in advance. If we don't do this, we can expect them to see our discipline as irrational, ill conceived, or even spiteful, and they won't learn much from it.

It is sensible to take away television privileges when children don't obey rules regarding time management or the sequence of work and pleasure. For example, if they play outside before their homework is done, they will naturally have to do their homework in the time they would normally watch television.

Rose Bushes also respond well to punishments they devise themselves. We can involve them in compiling the rules and determining the punishments for breaking them. I've often heard Rose Bushes come up with weightier consequences than I would have chosen. They are tough, and if a punishment is too light, they will assume you don't mean business.

6. Competitions, challenges, and records: Winning, or at least doing better than someone else, is so important to a Rose Bush that we can use this incentive in our discipline. Gold stars or stickers placed on a chart work well when an element of competition is added

between the Rose Bush and her siblings who also enjoy competition (most likely those with Palm or Rose in their personality), or when faced with the challenge of reaching the target within a set limit of attempts or time.

Better yet, let your Rose Bush compete against herself. Keep a written record to show how swiftly your Rose Bush is ready for school after getting up. Every time she tops her own record, she gets a point. When she has scored five points, extend her bedtime by fifteen or thirty minutes. If she starts being late for school again (usually because of fights about clothes, hair, or breakfast), the whole process starts over with her original bedtime. Friends of ours have a daughter who is a brilliant swimmer. She quickly rose to the top in her swimming club, and her dad took her to practice with a college team that had a few Olympic candidates. He thought the tough competition would motivate her. After the first practice, he eagerly asked if there was any competition for her there. She gave the ultimate Rose Bush answer: "Not in my lane, Dad."

7. Money: Rose Bushes react well to financial rewards because they like to cooperate when doing so has direct advantages for them.

The allowance of any child should at least be partly linked to his responsibilities in and around the house. It should be a matter of principle that money is not based on age but has to be earned. Children should also have a few chores for which they are not paid any money. They may be afforded opportunities to earn extra money, within limits, if the parents can afford it.

Be mindful of manipulation with money. Once you have determined a price, it should not be open to negotiation. If you're prepared to pay three dollars for cleaning the swimming pool, your child may decide that it's not worth it, and you'll find yourself doing the job. As parents, though, we have the right to demand that they do it, then give them three dollars as a token of appreciation. A child is allowed to refuse the money but not the responsibility! If the job is theirs and you usually pay them, they owe you money when they neglect that chore and leave you to do it.

Also be careful about things a Rose Bush might try to get you to pay for. One Rose Bush's mother told me once that her son was always willing to eat all his food for fifty cents, but one day when they were having dinner with people his mother was trying to impress, he saw an opportunity to increase his price. He wouldn't touch his food before his mother agreed to pay two dollars. This is a good example of how money should not be used! Eating one's food is not a job and therefore doesn't deserve pay.

Never try to buy obedience. Obedience is the least that we may demand from our children. If we subtracted a dollar from their allowance every time they disobeyed, we would be putting a very low price on obedience!

Make sensible plans about what you want to reward financially, and which losses of income your Rose Bushes can expect when they break the house rules. Use real life as a barometer. Nobody gets paid for arriving at work on time, but people do get a raise when they do more than is expected. Make it clear, reach a consensus beforehand, then stick to the agreement.

8. The broken-record technique: This technique works well with Rose Bushes and Palm Trees who protest, argue, or negotiate endlessly. It takes away the negotiation table at which they want to keep you. It is at odds, however, with the idea of making just one request

and then meting out punishment for not obeying. Therefore, this technique is better suited to parents who refuse to spank or punish and are looking for an alternative. Instead of reacting to defiance or manipulative behavior, you repeat the instruction word for word, like a broken record, without even changing your tone of voice or facial expression. Repeat the instruction as many times as necessary, but don't say anything else or react to anything else your Rose Bush is doing to sidetrack you! The message sent by this technique is that nothing is going to change, no matter the argument. The conversation may follow this pattern:

> Dad: "Son, please pack away the toys. It's time for bed."
> Child: "But I like to build towers on my bed, and I still want to build them."
> Dad: "It's time for bed."
> Child: "I said I don't feel like it now."
> Dad: "It's time for bed."
> Child: "It will take too long!"
> Dad: "It's time for bed."
> Child: "Okay, but I'm very angry with you now!"
> Dad: (silence—clever dad doesn't take the bait)

A CULTIVATION PLAN FOR ROSE BUSHES

We have already discussed in detail the firm hand needed for Rose Bushes. They prick us with those vicious thorns when we prune them, and they resist all our attempts at shaping them because they are so willful and determined. However, eventually we will be rewarded with beautiful roses—once those buds on the thorny branches open!

We should start by not biting off more than we can chew. We will have to choose the disciplinary targets for our Rose Bushes carefully to ensure we can stay in the battle until the very end. We also have to make sure we have a rich source of positive motivators to give our Rose Bushes so we not only prune but also water, because especially toddlers can become oppositional when we seem to clamp down on them without noticing their good side. Parenting becomes negative when we think that punishment corrects all behavior. Rose Bushes like punishing their parents, and our first instinct is to punish them right back. However, they need a crook as well as a stick. Shepherds use a stick to lightly whip their sheep to avert them from danger, but they also use a crook to hook them and direct them back onto the right road.

The following plan to change behavior can be used effectively with Rose Bushes. Begin by making three lists in the following table of things you want to work on.

To Do Less	To Do More Often	Doing Great!

What does my Rose Bush do too often or incorrectly?

You may write: She goes where she wants without asking, shouts at me, tosses or breaks things, throws tantrums in shopping centers or other public places, says no every time I give her an instruction, questions everything I say, and treats me without any gratitude or respect.

What does my Rose Bush do too infrequently or not at all?

Your list may include the following: He doesn't say please or thank you, doesn't answer when I instruct him to do something, refuses to get dressed, and doesn't clean up his toys at night.

What does my Rose Bush do right or often enough?

You may observe: She remembers to brush her teeth at night, faithfully waters the house plants, hands in school assignments on time, is back home by curfew, and finishes things she starts.

Now rank each type of behavior according to how urgently you need to attend to it. Mark the highest priority with a 1, and so forth.

Choose only one behavior from each list to start with.

Enlist helpers. Grandma, the teacher, brothers, sisters, caregivers, or your spouse can help by all expecting the same behavior from your child when he is in their care. For example, everybody should insist on a respectful answer; otherwise, the Rose Bush may treat you with respect but keep disregarding other authority figures.

Decide on a realistic time frame for each goal. Practicing asking permission may work well when you are on vacation because it offers many opportunities where your child can't just take what she wants or go off on her own. Decide more or less how long every objective will take to ensure that you give enough time for proper practice. It can take a month to learn to say thank you and please, two weeks to learn to say "Yes, Dad" when an instruction is given, and maybe longer to break the habit of automatically saying no to every instruction. As soon as one of these objectives is achieved, move on to number 2 on the list of priorities in the same column, so as never to have more than three challenges simultaneously demanding your attention.

Think about the behavior in the first column. Why does the Rose Bush do it? Which rewards does it have? How can you eliminate the rewarding element? How can you ensure in a justified, meaningful way that the behavior actually has negative consequences? What behavior do you expect instead? How can you reward the required behavior once your child starts behaving well?

Take, for example, the child who runs off without telling anyone or asking permission. Perhaps your child's "reward" is that you usually start searching and screaming hysterically. The Rose Bush enjoys your hysteria and the hide-and-seek game. (Yes, to the Rose Bush it can be a delightful power trip.) He also enjoys the space and freedom of the big park or supermarket. He might also receive a lot of attention when you find him. Make a deal that he will be rewarded with freedom and attention if he stays with you or asks permission before he goes off, but he will be punished when he doesn't do these things. Have him practice staying by your side without being held. If he can stay with you for the duration of your trip, reward him by playing a game of hide-and-seek at home or taking him to the park. If he runs off, calmly find him, then hold his hand or put him in the shopping cart for the rest of the trip.

"You get lost in this big space, so I need to keep you safe in a small space."

Even teenagers can experience the natural consequences of running off. The child who disappears just before dinnertime will not have a plate of food waiting in the oven, effectively rewarding her for disappearing by dealing with the implications on her behalf. For a teen, set a trial period of a month. If the behavior changes satisfactorily (the teenager notifies you of her movements for a whole month), she has earned more freedom.

Think about the behavior on the second list. Why doesn't my child do what I want him to do? Does my Rose Bush really know what I expect? Is the behavior I expect realistic given my child's age and abilities? Should my child perhaps be trained a lot more before this behavior will become a habit? How can I help my child succeed rather than just test him? Does he simply forget? If so, how can I help him remember?

Consider a young child who doesn't say please or thank you, though you believe she's old enough to do this without prompting. You want to find a way to impress it on her until it becomes automatic. First, tell her why you expect politeness. Then explain how things are going to work. When she remembers to say please or thank you on her own, she gets a point (which, for example, can be indicated on a reward chart). When she doesn't remember, you simply might say "Excuse me?" to prompt a response or take back the item you've just given (no point earned).

Think about the behavior on the third list, and decide how you're going to reward it. Review the "Develop" section for techniques and rewards that motivate Rose Bushes.

Saddle up and follow through with your choices. Remember that Rose Bushes will likely resist you trying to change their behavior. Therefore, treat it as their victory when they meet a challenge. Often say things like, "You are making good choices. You are coming along nicely. It seems that you are going to win the fight against bad manners."

DISCIPLE — SHAPING THE ROSE BUSH'S CHARACTER FOR GOD'S PURPOSE

Rose Bushes often become God's pioneers into tough new territories. They fight good fights, break new ground, and bring truth and direction to chaos and confusion. They can be apostolic and prophetic too! Our son is often on the receiving end of his younger sister's Rose Bush thorns. His conclusion was probably spot on: "God must have a very tough task for her in this world!" It's not fun being practiced on, though, so we have pruning to do yet.

The attitudes and skills below will be worth all the energy we invest in patiently and persistently teaching them to our Rose Bushes. Prayerfully insist on the behavior even when they resist, because even some grown-up Roses I know often do not feel like being nice. They do, however, *choose* to be, because they know their witness depends on it and the people they lead deserve it!

1. Valuing others, their feelings, and their viewpoints: Rose Bushes usually have so much self-confidence that it borders on arrogance, and they often don't see their own shortcomings. Ironically, other people's shortcomings are clear to them, and they easily look down on those who are weaker, smaller, slower, or different. Take

time to teach them that every person has value, talents, and short-comings. This doesn't mean one person is better than another.

Rose Bushes must be taught to understand that their actions and words affect other people. Tell them straight up when they've been hurtful because they may not be aware of it. Saying "I want to talk to you about how you make me feel" triggers them, as does the overly sweet voice and the stooping to their level that I've already advised against. When you whine, they hear weakness and want to put you out of your misery (or so they've told me).

Rose Bushes will defend their viewpoints with a vengeance if they're sure of themselves. My husband pointed this out in me and said, "Honey, you're often wrong but never in doubt." Teach Rose Bushes not to defend their viewpoints rudely but to say with respect, "I don't agree," or, "That is not what I saw."

2. Admitting mistakes and asking for forgiveness: Rose Bushes vehemently resist admitting guilt or mistakes. Be firm when dealing with this potential character flaw. Refuse to move on before your Rose Bush makes the necessary apology. For example, the Rose Bush may not continue playing until he has apologized to a friend for hurting him. He must apologize to the rest of the family for his outburst before he may continue with his meal. He must admit to Dad that the car was scratched and explain how it happened before he is allowed to use the car again.

Rose Bushes may need as much help with the wording of the apology as we would need with a foreign language. A good apology is offered even when we accidentally hurt someone, and it has four components: admitting what you have done, acknowledging what it did to the other person, expressing remorse, and asking for forgiveness. For example, "I tripped you. You really got hurt. I should have been more careful. Will you forgive me?"

3. Talking respectfully and tactfully: Rose Bushes often communicate cryptically and almost rudely. "I want bread." "Where is my gift?" "I don't want that food." "Go away." "Don't scold me." "Give me some too." It's a reasonable expectation that they talk in more acceptable ways. Rose Bush Christian leaders often lose their right to lead by breaking this rule. Your child is destined to lead, and his style of communication will define him.

Have your Rose Bushes practice saying someone's name first. They can build a better relationship with that person by saying please and thank you and using a soft tone of voice if they tend to bark. In our family we have a code phrase, "Try again," which means, "I have heard you and want to respond, but I won't be able to do that when you speak to me in such a way." It takes practice. A coaching session may sound like this:

> Rose Bush: (first words of the day) "Where's my cereal?"
>
> Mother: "Morning, Peter. First greet me."
>
> Rose Bush: "Hello."
>
> Mother: "Try again, Peter. Remember my name."
>
> Rose Bush: "Morning, Mom. I want my cereal."
>
> Mother: "You must be hungry. Try again by asking nicely."
>
> Rose Bush: "Mom, may I please have my cereal now?"
>
> Mother: "Of course, Peter. Let's go to the kitchen."

Rose Bush: "Don't pour so much milk over it."

Mother: "Try again."

Rose Bush: "Can you please pour less milk over it than yesterday, Mom?"

Mother: "I have an idea. You're big enough to pour your own milk. What do you think?"

Rose Bush: "Yes, give it here."

Mother: "Try again."

Rose Bush: "Please pass me the milk, Mom."

4. Servant leadership: Sometimes Rose Bushes can enjoy control and power over others so much that they completely forget how people must feel to be bossed around. As they grow older, discuss appropriate scriptures with them so they can see what kinds of leaders are good leaders in God's eyes. Use Ezekiel 34:1–10 as a guideline.

Choose at least one chore for the Rose Bushes in your house that requires them to help or serve other family members. For example: making Dad a cup of tea in the afternoon, sweeping the kitchen floor, washing the dishes, or looking after the baby. These chores may be met with resistance initially because Rose Bushes prefer doing things that benefit them directly.

5. Accepting help: Rose Bushes dislike asking other people for help and get angry or frustrated if they can't handle something on their own. If you try to help, they might meet you with ingratitude. This is why a Rose Bush toddler screams at the top of her voice, "Now, leave me alone! I want to do it!" even when we know she can't master the task herself. In these situations, we could say something like, "I see you are going to try again on your own. I can help if you

want. Just call me." When they keep refusing help, we can say, "You need help. Try one more time, then it's my turn." God takes Rose Bushes to the end of their abilities so their pride can be broken. To experience impossible challenges in childhood is a gift, and that is one of the ways Rose Bushes learn that they are not an island, and that it's not a sign of weakness to need others.

LET'S GET PRACTICAL

When people say we have to be "consistent," we often interpret it as follows: we need to act the same way in the same situation every time. If we have sent the child to his room for back-talking once, we have to send him to his room for back-talking every time, right? Not necessarily! Consistency doesn't necessarily require the same action on our part but rather requires having consistent *expectations* that result in predictable consequences. These consequences must be logical and instructive, and our actions in response to our child's misbehavior must be predictable. When I eat too much, I expect consistent results: the scale will show it! I don't expect my hair to fall out. Similarly, a child who takes something that doesn't belong to him should expect to give up something that would have been his—that is consistency. To make him sit in the bathroom and think about his sins is not consistent because it has nothing to do with his transgression. It doesn't teach him anything about the impact of his behavior, nor does it guide correct behavior in the future.

Consider the punishments or consequences in each scenario below, and try to choose the most logical consequence that could teach real-life consequences and skills. Compare your answers to another adult's answers, or mine, which I provide at the end of the exercise.

Can you spot the cruel punishments that will needlessly hurt the child; unfair punishments that have nothing to do with the offense; consequences that are too advanced for your child's age, abilities, reasoning skills, or moral development; actions that save your child from consequences; and those actions that could lead to the same behavior being repeated, continued, or worsened?

1 The six-year-old Rose Bush has knocked a glass from the table. It shatters into pieces, and milk is spilled on the carpet. This is the third time this week it has happened!

a. Make a new rule that she will not get something to drink at the table again until she is old enough not to knock over glasses. When she is thirsty, she has to get a drink in a plastic cup and finish it in the kitchen.

b. Give her rubber gloves, a dustpan and brush, and a floor cloth, and let her help you clean up. Put a brightly colored coaster in front of her plate as a reminder of where to put her glass.

c. Give her a spanking, because she has not learned from her previous two accidents. You warned her not to put her glass near the edge of the table, and therefore she has had enough chances now.

    d. Let her do chores in the house to earn money to replace the glass.

2. The four-year-old promised to tidy up his room before you read him a story at bedtime. When you ask him whether he did it, he answers, "Yes, Dad!" but upon further investigation you find that he just swept everything under the bed.

    a. You take out the toys from under the bed and lock them away for a week so that he can learn to take better care of his toys.

    b. You forbid him to play with those toys the next day, and you make him pack away all his other toys neatly the next evening.

    c. You give him a spanking because he lied to you and lies are a serious matter.

    d. You let him put the toys in the right places, and because it took extra time, and because he lied, there will be no story at bedtime today.

3. Your twelve-year-old went to visit a friend, and when you arrived early to pick her up, you saw that there were no adults at the house and the children were watching a film with an age restriction.

    a. You wait for the parents to come home and confront them because it is actually their fault that there was no supervision; and therefore, your child should not be punished. However, you do discuss age restrictions on the way home.

b. You make a rule that your child will not be allowed to visit that friend's home in the future and only invite the friend to your house under your supervision.

c. You use some of your child's allowance to rent the same film and expect her to watch it with you and discuss the content critically. She must also suggest a satisfactory plan for when adults leave the house and when friends suggest unhealthy or illegal entertainment.

d. Your child is not allowed to watch any television, videos, or movies for a month so that she can realize that it is a privilege that should not be abused.

4. Your two-year-old Rose Bush nags incessantly for ice cream after the ice-cream truck drives past your home.

a. You give him a spanking because you have said no three times and he refuses to stop crying.

b. You say "not ice-cream time" clearly and take him into the house in a firm but friendly manner. If you suspect he is really hungry, you wait for him to stop crying, then give him something healthy to eat instead.

c. You tell him he must stop crying, then you buy him an ice cream so that he can learn that he gets nothing when he cries but that he gets what he wants when he stops crying.

d. You explain to him why he is not allowed to have it. It is almost dinnertime, he is sensitive to dairy, he has eaten too much sugar already today, and it makes him hyperactive, and so on. Then you stick to your guns and refuse to buy it.

5. Your eleven-year-old fails her Business Economics test. After a while it turns out that she temporarily misplaced the book from which she was supposed to study.

a. You expect her to tell the teacher what happened and ask to retake the test or do an assignment to supplement her grades.

b. You ground her for a week because she didn't look after her books.

c. You do nothing because you feel she has learned her lesson to be more organized. The poor grades are punishment enough.

d. You let her spend extra hours studying Business Economics because she needs an 80 percent in classwork to make up for the low test score. If she doesn't manage to do that, she will be punished more severely.

6. Your eleven-year-old Rose Bush leaves a trail of dirty dishes, toys, and clothes everywhere in the house and back-talks when you reprimand him.

a. You take away his screen-time privileges until his tidiness improves.

b. You force him to stay home every Saturday to do some washing, clean the kitchen, and tidy up all his school things unless he doesn't let anything lie around for the whole week.

c. You explain that you will clean up after him, but as payment for your trouble, you will deduct a quarter from his allowance for each item you find out of place.

d. You donate the clothes that lie around to charity, wash none of his dishes or laundry, and hide his toys that lie around until he can learn to be neat.

7. Your ten-year-old frequently sneaks food from the cupboard, then lies if you ask her about it.

a. You make a new rule that she has to tell you when she is hungry. When she does this, you will always say yes to a tasty but healthy snack and to a small treat after dinner. If she takes snacks without asking, she will lose the treat and all snacks until dinner.

b. Every time you catch her, she has to apologize to the whole family for taking something that actually belongs to everyone. That will teach her that lies bring shame on her and that it is wrong to lie.

c. She must pay for everything she takes. You write down everything that "disappears" and then give her a "bill" at the end of the week to replace everything she took.

d. If you catch her, she must share with you what she took so she doesn't develop a pattern of eating alone secretly.

My answers: 1b, 2d, 3c, 4b, 5c, 6c, 7a.

CHAPTER 6

PARENTING THE BOXWOOD TREE

Read this chapter if your child tested Boxwood Tree, Box-Palm, Box-Rose, Box-Pine, or Contra-Palm. These trees are all in the Boxwood Tree family. Also read chapter 9 if your child is not a "pure" Boxwood Tree.

In this chapter:

- Meet Josh, a natural Boxwood Tree.
- Develop—how to nurture the nature of a young Boxwood Tree.
- Direct—what and how to teach a Boxwood Tree.
- Dialogue—how to speak the Boxwood Tree dialect.
- Discipline—how to train the Boxwood Tree way.
- Disciple—shaping the Boxwood Tree's character for God's purpose.

A boxwood is a stylishly pruned tree that is often used as decoration. These trees appear neat and tidy and controlled. The people represented by this tree have high standards and seem almost perfect to others. They can, like a boxwood in a pot, easily thrive in situations with strict rules and regulations. It is easy to shape them and they like boundaries. Hedges are often made out of boxwoods planted close together. Boxwood stems are sometimes made into chess pieces and tuning pins for musical instruments. And the Boxwood Tree personality is like a chess piece—moving only in the designated way, careful to keep to the rules, and not without first scanning the "playing field" for every trap and possibility.

MEET JOSH, THE NATURAL BOXWOOD TREE

Josh is the younger brother of Rose Bush Kevin and has almost nothing in common with his bold and daring brother.

Even as a preschooler Josh was serious. As soon as he could count, he wanted to know how many points out of ten he would get for keeping a tidy room. Criticism and harsh words turned him into a weepy bundle for hours on end, and his parents realized that he had a fragile self-image and required a gentle approach.

His sensitivity toward others led him to be his mother's sounding board, even at a tender age. He was her shoulder to cry on when her father died. Josh only cried when he was alone in his room because he felt it was his duty to be there for his mother. He cried himself to sleep many nights.

Josh was an exemplary seven-year-old and instantly became the teacher's pet. Even though he was an introvert, he was also very polite. During second grade Josh didn't do well on one of his spelling tests. He tried his best to wipe out the Xs with a pen eraser but tore the page. Because a torn page was even worse than a bad grade, Josh "lost" his book. He had to redo all the work in a new book, but he didn't mind because it meant he could rewrite everything as neatly and perfectly as he had wanted to in the first place.

Josh often worried about the future. How would it be when his brother left the house in a year or two? Who would drive him to his extracurricular lessons? What would happen if World War III broke out when he was old enough to be a soldier? What if a solar flare took out Amazon's headquarters or the entire Internet? His mom did everything online. Would she lose her job then? Would they be poor? He noticed how she saved money whenever she could. She no longer filled the fuel tank every time she stopped at the filling station. First she checked her purse, then decided how much fuel she wanted. Nothing escaped his keen observation.

He didn't ask his mother if he could take up chess, even though he really wanted to. He felt that his needs were not important.

In the afternoons after school, Josh did his homework without being reminded. Then he often checked his brother's room to make sure Kevin was also doing his part. Josh constantly found fault with Kevin's room and the way he did things. Kevin jokingly called him Joshlock Holmes for this ability to spot what was out of place.

Josh's prominent Boxwood temperament predicts that he will take life very seriously and bear a heavy burden, even when life has a lot to offer him. He feels everything that happens is important. Little problems turn him into a bundle of nerves. He frequently feels overwhelmed and doesn't know where to start to deal with it.

Josh is probably going to perform well at high school. He will make his parents proud by doing his best and staying out of trouble.

The football players may frown on his creative, intellectual, and linguistic talents, but he will need only a few friends who share his values. It will not bother him to be excluded from the "in" crowd.

People will probably say these things about Josh someday:

- "We give you the work that we want to have done right."
- "Don't be so serious—live a little!"
- "Look on the bright side!"
- "Haven't we been over this (repeatedly)?"
- "You are so organized!"
- "I wish I had your discipline."
- "You are so good at what you do."

DEVELOP — HOW TO NURTURE THE NATURE OF A YOUNG BOXWOOD TREE

With each of you we were like a father with his child, holding your hand, whispering encouragement, showing you step-by-step how to live well before God, who called us into his own kingdom, into his delightful life.

1 Thessalonians 2:11–12

In your child's Tall Trees Kids Profile Report, tailor-made needs similar to these below will be listed as the Boxwood's "Fertilizer."

1. Daily reassurance of our love: Boxwoods are the most emotional of all the trees, and unfortunately, they are also very sensitive. Figuratively speaking, they save negative feedback on their hard drive and positive words on a flash drive that is easily misplaced. They need

PARENTING THE BOXWOOD TREE

us to show them how much we love them, like them, and are proud of them—every day! This reassurance of our love is especially necessary after they have misbehaved, failed, or disappointed us.

2. Constant encouragement: Boxwoods are quick to get despondent when they don't feel supported. They work hard and persistently because they want to give their best, but they can suddenly go up in a puff of smoke when all the demands (real and imagined) become overwhelming. They just want to know that we see how hard they try, that we believe in them, and that we are available every now and then when they need our help.

Brag about them, "gossip" good things about them, compliment and encourage them with written notes, because these proofs of our approval are much more believable to them than a directly spoken compliment, which many Boxwoods file in a folder labeled "highly suspicious."

3. Careful feedback on the quality of their work: Boxwoods can't easily distance themselves from their work. If we don't praise the project they did in nursery school or if we criticize them for coloring outside the lines, they will take it personally. If they usually receive two stars for their work but receive only one today, it can be crushing. A Boxwood experiences feedback on her work as feedback on her as a person. Praise and a score of ten out of ten in her workbook mean that she is excellent, you are happy with her, and she herself is a ten out of ten. There's no need to fear that the positive feedback will go to their heads, as they need it daily. I've heard many Boxwoods say, "Yesterday's achievement doesn't last long. I start every day at a zero."

4. A boost to their self-image: Because they notice their own negative traits first, Boxwoods often have low self-confidence. They

are prone to perfectionism, self-examination, and feelings of guilt, and on top of it all they frequently compare themselves to others. Boost their self-image in the following ways.

First, talk to them about what it means to have a calling. They were made with a special plan in mind. This plan is, first of all, that the Lord wants to love them—that is the basic plan and reason for each person's existence. However, there is another reason: the Lord has a unique task for them in this world. This should form the basis of every person's self-worth and self-image.

Talk to them about the hidden gifts of their temperament—excellence, a good work ethic, a love of fairness, teachability, thoughtfulness, and attention to detail, to name a few—so that they can value themselves. Also reassure them that they will be unnecessarily critical of themselves, owing to their temperament type. Their true image will therefore probably be better than the image they have of themselves.

Second, we can help them in the social arena by explaining that there is nothing wrong with having only one or two close friends, because it means they were made to have deeper, stronger friendships.

Third, we can help them be successful problem solvers by allowing them to find their own ways to set things right. They respond very well to an opportunity to rectify their mistakes. This relates to problem solving and is essential for their self-image.

Finally, create opportunities for them to show their thoughtful side. It can be simple things, such as reminding forgetful friends of the important items to bring to camp or writing a teacher a get-well note. Seeing how their gifts benefit others builds a sense of worth that is more lasting than the perceived worth from their achievements.

5. Clear, consistent rules: Boxwoods are the only trees that like rules. Even before a simple game, they want the rules made clear. Without boundaries they become uncertain and confused. The more details they have, the safer they feel. It suits them when someone else makes the rules, and they are usually more than willing to cooperate.

They get upset when the rules are changed, are not followed, don't apply to everyone, or are not taken seriously. They like to act as second-in-command by reminding everyone of the rules when the teachers or parents are away.

6. Help with priorities: Everything is equally important—vitally important!—to a Boxwood. They get tense over trivialities: when their assignment is one page longer or shorter than the teacher said it had to be, when they can't find one of their puzzle pieces, or when they haven't received a testing schedule a month before final exams. There is always something to worry about. Sometimes simple questions help, such as: Which task will take the longest to complete? Which assignment has to be handed in first? What do you need to finish that assignment? Who can help you with this? What do you think the first step of this assignment should be?

7. Early warnings of changes and major events: A Boxwood wakes up with a schedule in her head, with everything she has to do or plan to accomplish already mapped out. When we suddenly disturb her normal routine, everything seems disrupted and she loses her feeling of security.

Boxwoods might welcome changes such as a new house or the birth of a sibling, but they hate changes to their school schedules, deadlines, or changes in stated requirements because they aren't sure how these will affect their performance.

8. Routine, information, schedules, frameworks, lists, watches, and calendars: Like Rose Bushes, Boxwoods also like being in control, but they're more concerned with having control over their own lives than over other people or events. From early childhood they welcome a predictable, set routine. The more details they have in black and white, the better. The older they get, the more Boxwoods love these types of organizational resources.

If our Boxwoods tend to get anxious, we can help them by building this kind of structure into their lives. Put up a schedule or calendar that indicates the whole family's weekly activities and other important dates to keep them in the loop.

9. An opportunity to make up for mistakes: Boxwoods have sensitive consciences from an early age. They typically feel sincere regret when they are wrong. They blame and punish themselves with self-reproach. We have to help them forgive themselves. Allow them to try to make up for their mistakes. Let them clean up spills and messes themselves, then try again. When they apologize, accept the apology in love.

10. Quiet me-time: Boxwoods need time alone daily. They find it hard to orient themselves properly in noisy or busy environments. If possible, the Boxwood should not have to share a room with siblings, especially if the roommate is messy. If there is no alternative, their privacy should be respected as much as possible. Their toys should at least be kept separate. While other kids may experience being sent to their room as punishment, Boxwoods could be relieved to have permission to take a breather in their own space!

11. Discovery and development of creative talents: Boxwoods are often artistic. One should give them the opportunity to master

at least one musical instrument or art form. This will give them a way to build their fragile self-image. However, exams and competitions, concerts, art exhibitions, recitals, and expos should not be the focus—unless they are naturally competitive because of a bit of Rose Bush in their mix. Consider these activities for personal therapy, not for showing off in public.

12. Opportunity to cope with their intense emotions in their own time: Boxwoods' experiences are intense, and their emotional reactions to events can last a long time. Unfortunately, they can't be cheered up or distracted easily once they feel sad or despondent. Their emotions deserve to be handled with extreme tenderness. This aspect is vital, because disregarding Boxwoods' emotions is equal to disregarding them as people.

Feelings never need to be "fixed." In fact, feelings are never "broken."
Dr. Lloyd J. Thomas, "Understanding Your Emotions"

We can't help Boxwoods on a rational level with their emotions; we have to meet them on an emotional level. Here are some skills parents need to help a Boxwood with her emotions:

Try to acknowledge your Boxwood's experience of the situation rather than looking at the situation as you see it. If the Boxwood thinks that broken swimming goggles is a national crisis, don't immediately offer to buy a new pair. He wants you to mourn his loss with him.

Acknowledge the emotion, even if you think it is unfounded. A Boxwood wants your understanding, not your advice or appeasement. Say something like, "It upsets you when something breaks. That's why you're crying about the broken goggles."

Arguments won't change the situation. When a Boxwood teenager is crushed after a failed relationship, avoid clichés and cold facts like "There are plenty of fish in the sea. After all, only 5 percent of people marry their high school sweetheart." Reason won't change the way she feels. When a Boxwood is emotional, the rational part of her brain shuts down completely! Agree with her instead: "It's very painful to lose that special bond with someone."

An emotional Boxwood doesn't want to answer many questions. Asking in an annoyed tone, "How did you manage to break the goggles? Where did you leave them?" will only infuriate him or add to the shame he already feels.

If the emotion stays intense, despite your understanding and calm acknowledgment, your Boxwood probably wants time and privacy to work through it, so give her space. Walk away with friendly words, such as, "Later, when you feel better, we can talk if you like. I am sorry you're feeling so sad."

There is nothing sweeter than to be sympathized with.
George Santayana, *Little Essays Drawn from the Writings of George Santayana*

DIRECT — WHAT AND HOW TO TEACH A BOXWOOD TREE

Our Boxwoods need to learn:

1. To set realistic standards for themselves and others: Boxwoods can easily lose perspective and decide, for example, that they want to raise their marks by 20 percent in one school term, or that they want to achieve a perfect score for a specific assignment. If they don't succeed, they may be crushed. Teach them to take

baby steps by setting smaller goals that add up to something they feel is significant.

They're often unrealistic about how many things they want to get done. Help them decide which are the most helpful and important. Assure them that they don't need to do everything on their list in one day, or they'll wear themselves out.

Perfection can become their slave master. Emphasize creativity and originality above a faultless result. Show them the beauty in the imperfect brushstrokes on a canvas and in the freckles on a gorgeous face, so that they can discover how imperfect details can still be part of an acceptable whole. Teach the value of "good enough."

> *The principle mark of genius is not perfection, but*
> *originality, the opening of new frontiers.*
> Arthur Koestler, *The Act of Creation*

2. To replace negative self-talk with positive self-talk: Explain to your child that thoughts are like a ladder. Each time we think a thought, we go one step up or down the ladder. When we think negative thoughts, we go down, and it becomes darker and darker; when we think positively, we go up and one step closer to the sunlight. Our brains and bodies "listen" to the words we say to ourselves, and we get sick and stressed when our words to ourselves aren't full of hope. Teach your Boxwood a few phrases he can repeat to himself when negative emotions threaten to take over:

- Jesus and your parents will still love you, even when you make mistakes.

- When you learned how to ride a bike, it was hard, but now you're a pro. Most hard things become easy if you keep trying.
- The words of that person don't count. Only words of people who love you count.
- How do you want to feel? You can choose. Thinking right can help you feel better!
- You can choose how long to stay discouraged. Decide when you want to put it behind you. (This is something one should never say to a Boxwood; a Boxwood can say it to himself, though!)

3. To label emotions: When a Boxwood is overcome by emotions, she can't always explain what she feels or why she is feeling that way. Naming the emotions gives your child a handle on them. When we use the techniques I mentioned earlier, we can help her reflect on her emotions: "I see you're disappointed" or "You seem angry to me" or "It seems as if you're frustrated." When we don't sum up the emotion correctly, the Boxwood will probably react with something like, "No, that's not it," or, "You don't understand." Keep quiet then so she can try to explain. If the Boxwood doesn't say anything else, perhaps it is wise to accept that and just say something like, "I see it's hard for you and I hope you can sort it out," and leave it at that.

It's often easier for Boxwoods to write down their feelings. If your Boxwood can write, encourage her to keep a journal.

Teach Boxwoods to think about their feelings in what Gary Smalley calls "emotional word pictures."[12] It is a valuable way to make someone understand how deep the feeling of hurt is. After a conversation in which I inadvertently insulted my son, he said, "I feel like a candle blown out, and will need time to light my own flame again." It said so much more than just, "You hurt me, Mom."

4. To console themselves: Boxwoods often experience our attempts to console them as disapproval or disregard of them and their emotions. They feel our intolerance of their mood. Understanding the intensity of their emotions is much more important to them than comforting or consoling them. They want compassion, not a solution. Maybe they even want to cry! Only they can actually console themselves, but we can help them find the techniques that work best for them. Some need to sit in their rooms and have a good cry; others need a walk outside. Some are consoled by listening to their favorite music or holding their favorite teddy bears. Make suggestions, and let your Boxwood experiment with them. Note what works, and tell him what you see; for example, "I saw how stroking the cat made you feel better. I feel better when I take off my shoes and lie down a little with my eyes closed."

5. To give people the benefit of the doubt regarding their intentions: Boxwoods often assume the worst in any unpleasant situation. They are quick to turn into self-pitying victims. When someone hurts them, they tend to believe it was on purpose. When someone forgets to tell them something, they may believe it's because this person doesn't like them anymore and excluded them intentionally.

Boxwoods believe themselves to be rational, but in fact their emotions often lead them to the wrong conclusions in conflicts. Teach them to get the facts from the other person by asking directly if there is something wrong and if they are reading the situation correctly. Even a small child can be taught to simply ask, "Are we still friends, or are you mad at me?" rather than assuming that the friend who doesn't want to play hates her.

6. To serve others when they themselves are feeling down: Boxwoods can be selfish and self-sacrificing at the same time. Sometimes, as adults, they have wonderful service-oriented careers and become volunteer community workers, provided they are encouraged to live outside of their comfort zones. They should be exposed to the needs of others from a young age, or they could get so caught up in their own concerns that their compassion for others gets drowned out.

The parents of a young Boxwood with terminal cancer understood this characteristic of their child and bought her a puppy. Taking care of this helpless being enabled her to look away from her own helplessness.

7. To relax: Many Boxwoods are constantly serious and slightly stressed. When anything goes against what they regard as the "right way" based on their beliefs, it is hard to convince them that it's not a big deal. Yolanda, mom of five-year-old Boxwood Linay, learned this at the dinner table one night. Linay learned about the stomach in preschool that day. When Yolanda dished up food, Linay got upset, held up her small fist, and said, "Mom, my tummy is only as big as my fist. You've dished up too much food for me! Mommy's wasting our money!" It probably took a lot of patient assurance that they could afford the food and that her tummy could stretch before Linay ate her dinner.

As their school years become busier, Boxwoods need to be taught to put worries and work aside, even if only for a few minutes. Sometimes it helps them to put aside something symbolic. Maybe they can simply write down or draw all their worries about tomorrow and all their painful memories of the day in a diary or journal before bedtime. When they close the book, they can visualize a door shutting between them and those things so they can sleep peacefully. Praying and telling God about each concern often makes the difference between a sleepless night and a peaceful one.

Note nervous habits and stress-related behaviors in your Boxwood, and help him find ways to make the butterflies in his stomach at least fly in unison, if they can't settle completely! Slight anxiousness is normal for Boxwoods. They use it as fuel to keep going. It is a concern only when they are unable to relax between stressful times.

8. To get to know themselves: Because Boxwoods want to make other people happy, play by the rules, and do everything perfectly, they can easily end up living their whole lives for others without ever asking, "What do I enjoy? What would I like to do?" Before long they can be left with one agonizing question: "Who am I?" Help them answer this question by observing them closely and as objectively as possible, giving feedback on what you observe: "I see you enjoy horseback riding even when the horse is obstinate" or "It seems to me that your favorite pastimes during the holidays were painting and drawing." By assembling these remarks into a picture of their true selves, Boxwoods can break through the molds of other people's expectations to be who they really are and what they are destined to become.

Our Boxwoods learn best:

- when parents and teachers are gentle and friendly
- when they are allowed to ask questions until they understand

- when there are written instructions or visual information
- by starting a task alone before someone else joins in
- when they have ordered surroundings
- when the end goal, the method, and the sequence are clear
- when they are allowed to make mistakes and rectify them
- from a role model who is qualified and has the same high standards they have

DIALOGUE — HOW TO SPEAK THE BOXWOOD TREE DIALECT

How does God speak to Boxwoods?

The LORD said, "I have indeed seen the misery of my people in Egypt. I have heard them crying out because of their slave drivers, and I am concerned about their suffering. So I have come down to rescue them from the hand of the Egyptians and to bring them up out of that land into a good and spacious land, a land flowing with milk and honey—the home of the Canaanites, Hittites, Amorites, Perizzites, Hivites and Jebusites. And now the cry of the Israelites has reached me, and I have seen the way the Egyptians are oppressing them. So now, go. I am sending you to Pharaoh to bring my people the Israelites out of Egypt…. But I know that the king of Egypt will not let you go unless a mighty hand compels him. So I will stretch out my hand and strike the Egyptians with all the wonders that I will perform among them. After that, he will let you go. And I will

make the Egyptians favorably disposed toward this people, so that
when you leave you will not go empty-handed. Every woman is to
ask her neighbor and any woman living in her house for articles
of silver and gold and for clothing, which you will put on your
sons and daughters. And so you will plunder the Egyptians."

Exodus 3:7–10, 19–22 NIV

Now go; I will help you speak and will teach you what to say.

Exodus 4:12 NIV

Moses was a classic Boxwood. The first words used by the Lord
to announce Moses's calling connect with his sadness. Moses's compassion for his people was the reason he was in the desert, but it was
also the reason why God chose him to lead his people out of Egypt.
The Lord also saw the people's suffering (Exodus 3:7–10).

The Lord approaches Boxwoods more gently than He does Rose
Bushes or Palm Trees, with not so much thunder, lightning, and
majesty (Exodus 3:1–4).

The Lord repeatedly tells Moses how everything will work
out. Moses knows beforehand how the story will end—something
a Boxwood appreciates (Exodus 3:19–22). When Moses expresses
doubts, the Lord repeats everything and reassures him with promises
(Exodus 6:1–8; 7:1–5).

The Lord prepares Moses for every big crisis by telling him
what is going to happen and how He will come to Moses's rescue. A
Boxwood doesn't naturally have the inner strength to follow blindly
and walk into the lion's den without such guarantees and encouragement to hold on to (Exodus 14:1–4; Numbers 14:27–35).

The Lord cheers Moses on when he feels inadequate and assures him of His help (Exodus 3:12; 4:12; 7:1).

The Lord talks to Boxwoods in great detail because they remember the detail, or they write it down and convey it carefully to those they have to teach (Exodus 21–23; 24:3–4, 7; 25–32).

The Lord helps the Boxwood gain perspective and avoid getting caught up in unimportant details (Luke 10:41).

The Lord reveals His majesty in words to Boxwoods so they can remember who He is and draw strength from that when they feel tired or weak (Exodus 34:5–7; John 11:25–26).

How should we talk to our Boxwoods?

Because we want our Boxwoods to understand what we say, we can follow these guidelines:

A Boxwood listens to the way we speak (emotions), and not only to what we say. We'd do well to communicate calmly and in a friendly manner. They detect negativity quickly, and we can expect a hurt and even hurtful reaction. When we whine, they do too.

Boxwoods love having important information in writing. Make sketches of rules and put them up where the Boxwood can refer to them.

They want to feel appreciated. Therefore, say please and thank you when your expectations require effort on their part. Saying, "I know you would rather have stayed until the end of the concert. Thank you for leaving on time for your curfew" will help an annoyed Boxwood deal with the disappointment of missing the last song.

Boxwoods need to understand everything in detail, so repeat what you said patiently when necessary.

Convey that you understand the emotion that your Boxwood is experiencing by saying, "I realize that this instruction [or punishment or request or word] makes you feel _____."

Beware of saying things that could convey disregard for your Boxwood's intense emotions and experiences. Forbidden phrases include: Get a grip. Stop crying. Get over it. How long are you going to keep on sulking? What is so bad about that? Tomorrow is another day. Don't worry; other people are worse off than you. Be grateful—it could have been much worse. I know of someone who ...

Remember that Boxwoods tend to hear the negative. Avoid following up a compliment with criticism. When we tell Boxwoods, "The room looks nice, but next time remember to close the closet door," they only hear, "Your closet door should have been closed."

Be sure of your facts and talk privately when you think they are guilty. When reprimanded in public, they get defensive and will probably lie to protect their self-image or cite proof that they are not wrong.

If Boxwoods do something wrong that we didn't expect of them, try not to overreact. Question them to discover the reason behind the behavior. When they break rules, there typically is more to the situation than meets the eye. My usually well-behaved daughter once cut all our living room blinds into different lengths. She still stood with scissors in hand when I caught her. My assumption was that she was downright destructive, but a few questions revealed the real motive: the blinds were very boring, and she was merely doing interior decoration. She loved them more this way and thought I would too, hence the evidence everywhere. She felt proud, not guilty.

Boxwoods often become uncharacteristically aggressive when criticized and can retaliate with razor-like sharpness. It is unwise to respond to the exact words they say then. They know they are unfair and will feel terrible about their words anyway. Rather, note the emotion, acknowledge their hurt, and ask for a chance to discuss it once everyone is calm. In that later conversation, make them aware of this tendency and suggest better ways to respond.

We can't take back nasty words once we have said them because Boxwoods remember everything! Every time I jokingly say they keep an alphabetic file of the things we say, with notes on the date and place we said it and what we were wearing at the time, several Boxwoods laugh and nod their heads. One Boxwood woman added, "And a backup file in case I lose the original!" When we have lashed out, attacked their character, or were unreasonable, we have to apologize. Perhaps then our entry in their file will be deleted.

Boxwoods are sensitive to nonresponsiveness because they fill the gaps of silence themselves. They tend to imagine the worst, may put words in your (closed) mouth, and usually imagine your anger or unhappiness to be far worse than it really is. If you don't know what to say, at least try to say, "I will tell you how I feel later; just give me time." Then keep your promise and respond in a reasonable time frame.

How can we listen to our Boxwoods better?

Remember that an emotional avalanche of words is part of the Boxwood's style—if the story seems confusing, listen to the heart.

Boxwoods see all details as equally important. Therefore, be patient while they go down many detours to get to their destination.

Ask them to summarize everything they have said if you know you missed the bottom line or if you lost concentration during a long story. If they think you have simply shut down, it hurts them immensely.

Boxwoods can immediately sense when you're critical or skeptical about what they're saying, and they'll become guarded. They'll avoid opening their hearts to you in the future. Be careful not to raise your eyebrows, frown, sigh, or give other negative nonverbal feedback while they're talking. Give them a chance to talk, then respond thoughtfully.

Understand that their many detailed questions don't indicate distrust in you. Boxwoods merely have an intense need to know and understand things.

Some Boxwoods like to complain and usually have a completely separate whiny voice for such occasions. You should never respond to that voice or it will become permanent. Say calmly, "I want to listen, but you will have to use your friendly voice."

Look out for the Boxwoods' secret weapons to manipulate parents—emotional complaining and unreasonable accusations. When you hear this, point it out and make sure that it doesn't become a pattern with your Boxwoods. They may cry genuine tears, but when those tears come with lyrics such as, "I just want to be with Jesus and then you will all be sorry!" the manipulation needs to be pointed out and nipped in the bud.

In summary:

- Be calm.
- Be specific.
- Be matter of fact.
- Be available to help.
- Be appreciative of their efforts.

DISCIPLINE — HOW TO TRAIN THE BOXWOOD TREE WAY

Each tree type has its own pruning and watering needs. These approaches work the best with Boxwoods:

1. Reaffirm the rules: Because Boxwoods accept rules, reminding them of a boundary or rule usually brings about the desired behavior immediately. An unemotional, "But you are not allowed to jump on the bed!" is sufficient for a typical Boxwood. Don't be surprised if you get a compliant answer: "Oh yes. I'm sorry, Mommy."

2. Do-overs: Because Boxwoods really want to do the right thing (according to their own perception of "right"), we could try to give them the chance to rectify their mistakes on their own. They sometimes have an excessive sense of fairness. Take it into account when choosing consequences. They'd prefer to mend something they broke rather than be scolded for breaking it.

3. Sincere encouragement: When they perform well or do something that pleases you, remember to give your Boxwoods recognition in their preferred way—a private rather than public reward. Boxwoods are shy when we praise them in front of others, but they appreciate it when we look them in the eyes and say something sincere, such as, "I notice that you are doing your best. It always pays to be dedicated."

4. Point systems and reward charts: Of all the tree types, the nature of a Boxwood makes her react most favorably to reward charts. Put one up on the wall of her room or inside her closet where it is not too public and reward her visibly with stars or points. It will defy your goal when you work negatively on such charts by taking away stars, deducting points, or sticking black dots on it. This visual reminder of failure is devastating to a Boxwood's confidence.

If it's difficult for you to maintain this kind of system, use a five-point system: one point each for brushing their teeth; putting the cap back on the toothpaste tube; rinsing their mouth, the brush, and the basin; returning the toothbrush and tube to the container; and having a pleasant attitude. You then only say something like, "Nice going. That was a four. Returning the cap too will give you a five," and your child can jot down the given points on the chart.

5. Loss of or increase in privileges: Boxwoods value privileges that are related to their need for privacy, creativity, order, and silence. They may be best rewarded by being allowed to spend time alone in their own rooms. (This type of "reward" would make a Palm Tree feel unloved!)

6. A thoughtful item: To receive something they are not required to share as a special reward is wonderful for Boxwoods. Items that help them organize their world and do well at their schoolwork or chores are hugely motivating too.

A CULTIVATION PLAN FOR BOXWOODS

Boxwoods are not really a disciplinary challenge, and their parents usually think more of their own abilities as parents than they ought to! The emotional challenge with raising Boxwoods is, however, enormous. They are not a handful, but rather a heartful. We worry about their self-image, not their marks, and about their fears, not their friends. We worry about not stepping on those long toes and wish we could talk to them without the tear ducts (or floodgates!) opening up wide. The most important step in the cultivation plan of Boxwoods is to know that we won't get anywhere with emotion—not theirs or our own. We need to create calm, or at least wait for it, before we proceed.

Boxwoods who are approached with metaphorical chainsaws or axes usually don't survive the discipline in their homes. Emotional and physical forcefulness can destroy these delicate saplings. Our cultivation plan should therefore include minimal or no spanking and healthy doses of kind words and other gentle approaches. Yet, although it will be difficult, we will still need to punish them sometimes.

Punishment plays a pivotal role in shaping a conscience, because it answers the inexperienced child's question: "Is this right or wrong, and if it is wrong, how serious is it?"
Dr. James Dobson, *The New Dare to Discipline*

The following plan to change behavior can be used effectively with Boxwoods. Begin by making three lists in the following table of things you want to work on.

To Do Less	To Do More Often	Doing Great!

What does my Boxwood do too often or incorrectly?
The list may include: talks in a whiny voice, bursts into tears every time I criticize, easily gets discouraged or frustrated, speaks

PARENTING THE BOXWOOD TREE

ill of other people, is full of whims and fancies regarding food, and accuses me of being unfair.

What does my Boxwood do too infrequently or not at all?

For example, he doesn't take care of his pet, doesn't eat his school lunch, doesn't bring home letters and report cards that are unfavorable, and doesn't appreciate what his parents do for him unless it is done exactly the way he wants it.

What does my Boxwood do right or often enough?

This list may include: does his homework conscientiously, is on time for school and meals, helps Mom around the house, completes his tasks, obeys the house rules, and keeps his room tidy. This list is essential so that we don't only nag about everything that is wrong but also focus on the good behavior of our Boxwoods, who get disheartened so quickly.

Now rank each type of behavior according to how urgently you need to attend to it. Mark the highest priority with a 1, and so forth.

Choose only one thing from each list to start with.

Explain your goals and plan to Grandma, the teacher, brothers, sisters, caregivers, or your spouse so that you can have consistent expectations regarding the behavior. For example, everybody should insist on a friendly tone instead of a whiny voice.

Decide on a realistic time frame for each goal, and pick the best time to start the training in new behavior patterns. It won't be wise to increase your Boxwood's stress levels just before final exams by adding new expectations! If the whole family has to cooperate, we would need to ensure that both parents are involved. As soon as your Boxwood achieves one of these objectives, move on to number 2 in the same column. Focus on no more than three challenges at the same time.

Think about the behavior in the first column. What is the Boxwood's reason for misbehaving? Which rewards does it hold? How can I take away the rewarding element? How can I ensure in a justified, meaningful way that it has negative consequences? With which behavior should she replace it? How can I reward the required behavior once my child starts behaving well?

Take, for example, the accusation that you behave unfairly toward him. Boxwoods love to make us feel guilty. They usually feel that they get the worst share of everything. The reward for their behavior is that it does indeed make the parents feel guilty or at least think about giving concessions to the disgruntled Boxwood. In this way our no frequently turns into a yes.

We may decide, for example, to work on this tactic for a month in the following way: We will make our Boxwood aware of his tendency to manipulate us. We will explain that we won't allow any manipulative behavior. If he accuses us of being unfair, he won't get what he wanted for a certain period of time. For example, if he says his sister is always allowed to go to the movies and he isn't, he will not be allowed to go to the movies for the next two weekends. When he truly feels grieved, he is not allowed to use this accusatory manner. He is, however, allowed to ask in a respectful, calm way, "What is the reason that I may not go to the movies but Sarah may?" After this, he needs to accept our explanation without trying to manipulate us further. When he succeeds in taking no for an answer without playing on our feelings, we'll give him credit for this and allow him a special privilege of his choice. For example, he may stay up later, invite a friend over, pick out a movie to watch at home, or choose what the family will have for dinner. When the month is over, there are no more special rewards for the correct behavior—only recognition and encouragement. The wrong behavior will mean that we have to follow the above plan again for another month.

Think about the behavior on the second list. Why doesn't my child do what I want him to do? Does he simply forget? If so, how can I help him remember? Does my Boxwood really know what I expect? Is the behavior I expect realistic given my child's age and abilities? Should my child perhaps have more opportunities to practice the correct behavior, and can I help her practice these skills?

Let's use the report cards as an example. The Boxwood probably fears consequences for poor grades or is simply ashamed of them. He doesn't mean to deceive or be dishonest, and we'll need a talk about expectations. We'd rather know where the schoolwork issues are than be in the dark and think that all is hunky-dory. He may need our assurance that he won't be punished for poor grades. Together we can make a plan to revisit the work he didn't understand or to have a tutor help him catch up.

Think about the behavior on the third list, and decide how you are going to reward it. The Boxwood will be unaware of everything he does right and needs positive reinforcement. I would definitely recommend a "brag chart" with stars or stickers for young Boxwoods. Describe the good behavior in clear terms on top; for instance, "Your room is an example! You have done your best! You are one in a million!" For older Boxwood children I suggest notes. Write a short letter showing what you see and appreciate about them, and put it where they will discover it, such as on their headboard or closet door.

Take the bull by the horns and follow through with your choices. Remember to stay as positive as possible. Make sure that this discipline plan is not the center of your relationship and communication. Talk about other things, and give lots of unconditional love, even when the plan is not going well. Your child is more than his successes or failures. Boxwoods in particular need to experience this truth.

DISCIPLE — SHAPING THE BOXWOOD TREE'S CHARACTER FOR GOD'S PURPOSE

Boxwood Trees fulfill many key roles in God's work in the world. They implement His principles, convey His teachings, establish His justice, and help His people in practical ways by working hard and faithfully. They also serve through their talents in music, arts, and language (one of which at least half of them possess). By nature, they serve but tend to complain as they do it or criticize those who don't do it "the right way." But when your parenting efforts in the areas below come together with God's Spirit, their hearts can change from law loving to grace loving, and they become blessings to everyone fortunate to know them!

1. Curb criticism and judgment: Boxwoods can be quite critical. If your Boxwood often criticizes others openly, you should intervene

and forbid such gossip or bad-mouthing. If the criticism becomes a judgmental attitude, it's on the verge of becoming an unattractive character trait. When the criticism is true, you may want to teach your Boxwood the principle of speaking only what is helpful and kindly put. It may be true that a certain person has poor table manners, but is it helpful in the situation to point it out? Also, when we feel we have to acknowledge a mistake, we'd do well to balance it out with a positive: "She lied to her friend. It is wrong, but I have seen her be very generous with her spending money."

2. Stop negative thought patterns and reverse them: When your Boxwood experiences disappointment, she'll start talking to herself about it: "If only I didn't do that! I am the only one who ever gets into this kind of mess. Surely nobody will want to help me. I know how this will end. I knew it would happen." These thoughts draw her deeper and deeper into an abyss of self-pity, despair, and even anger. You can teach your Boxwood how to think about bad experiences in a new and different way. Practice with your child to turn the situation around as follows:

Let your child sit back, relax, and close her eyes. Encourage her to picture the bad thing that happened as a still photo rather than a film that keeps playing. In this way she can choose one "frame" to control by "freezing" it. If she's old enough, let her remove all color from her picture so that the mental photo is black and white. She can even be encouraged to draw it.

If other people's words have hurt her, let her write new words for the people in the picture. The friend who had shouted, "I wish you would fall and break your neck!" could now say, "I am angry with you, but I will cool down again."

Let her change the picture as she likes—take away someone or put someone in, for example. If she could imagine her father being there, holding her hand while everything happened, she might feel safer than in the original memory. She could change the facial expressions if it would make her feel better.

Now let her describe the "new" situation as she sees it in her picture.

Do not let your hearts be troubled, neither let it be afraid. [Stop allowing yourselves to be agitated and disturbed; and do not permit yourselves to be fearful and intimidated and cowardly and unsettled.]
John 14:27 (AMP CLASSIC)

3. Accept people who think and act differently than they do: Boxwoods usually see things in black and white. They can be rigid and believe that only their way, perspective, or method is correct. Boxwoods often keep to the letter of the law when they are adults because they never learned to adjust their perspective when they were young. Boxwoods can be narrow minded and measure everyone according to their standards. They should be exposed to as much diversity as possible from a young age: Take them to experience different cultures, creeds, and communities. Interpret these encounters with them. Give them books to read about people from other sectors of society and from different cultures. When they learn to understand other people, Boxwoods can become the most compassionate and serving people on earth!

4. Forgive and forget: Unfortunately, Boxwoods automatically keep records of wrongdoings. Nobody can revive an old dispute

more quickly than some Boxwoods can. Boxwoods tend to live in the past and the future. They have remorse about the past and concern about the future, which can become a character flaw that can make Boxwoods unpopular and prevent them from having good relationships. Few people can maintain a relationship in which mistakes are seldom forgiven and forgotten. Therefore, we should refuse to allow them to dredge up the past, even when they are young. Teach your Boxwood the following things about forgiveness by giving examples from life:

- Everyone gets hurt.
- Everyone hurts other people and then needs to be forgiven.
- An unforgiving nature ties us to the person who has hurt us. If we forgive, we are also set free.
- When we don't forgive, we are saying that what Jesus did for us on the cross is not enough. Somebody else must add to it by being punished too. That is a little silly, isn't it? Didn't Jesus take everybody's punishment for every little wrong thing they would ever do?
- We can choose to believe that the nasty behavior was the result of the culprit's own emotional pain. When we remember that they are also hurting, it is easier to let go.
- We should not discuss things that have been forgiven because the test of true forgiveness is whether we still tell other people the story of our offense.

5. Ask for help, and spell out their needs: Boxwoods easily feel helpless, and unfortunately, they have trouble asking for help. We do them a favor when we teach the helpless bundle of self-pity to frequently ask, "Can you please help me?" and to answer the question, "How can I help you?" On the one hand they usually think that everyone should sort out their own problems, but on the other hand they feel that someone ought to help them, even if they don't ask for help. What a recipe for desperation!

Each time our Boxwoods express worry or discouragement (and that may be often), we have an opportunity to point out the Lord's love, care, and presence. Tell them from a young age that the Lord wants to be with them, can hear their cries, wants to help them, protects them with His angels, knows how they feel, and will never let go of them. Let them memorize Bible verses about these truths, and even post them in visible places such as the bathroom mirror. Once God's encouragement becomes a reality to them, they can pass on this hope to others!

LET'S GET PRACTICAL

Five of the eight statements or questions below would negate a Boxwood's feelings. Identify and replace these five with a statement or question that conveys empathy and understanding. Answers and alternative reactions are provided at the end of this exercise.

1. Don't feel so sorry for yourself.

2. You are not the only one who was hurt.

3. You have a very gentle spirit. That is precious.

4. I don't know what to do when you cry like that.

5. You can come and sit with me anytime, even if you are too sad to talk.

6. Laugh and the world laughs with you; cry and you cry alone.

7. Surely it can't be that bad!

8. Have you ever noticed that rude people upset you?

Answers/Alternatives:

1. It seems as if you feel you are suffering more than you deserve.

2. I think many people have experienced this and will agree with you that it is painful. I hope they will also have someone to talk to.

4. What can I do that will help you when you are so sad?

6. You are allowed to laugh and cry. We see that in the book of Psalms. All of us feel happy at times and sad at times.

7. I am sorry to see it was really hard for you. I wish it didn't hurt you so deeply.

Mark the communication mistakes listed below that you make with your Boxwood. Circle those that could cause your relationship to be shipwrecked, and work on replacing these with a communication habit that expresses your love for your Boxwood.

- I show my annoyance when he is emotional.
- I walk away when she cries because it upsets me.
- I show impatience with all the questions.
- I don't write any notes.
- I don't pay attention to details when he talks—it exhausts me.
- I don't give feedback when she does something for me.
- I discuss his faults with other people.
- I coerce or nag when she gets discouraged instead of encouraging her.
- I often forget to tell him that I love him.
- I often don't give enough timely information.
- I rush her when she tells a detailed story.

CHAPTER 7

PARENTING THE PINE TREE

Read this chapter if your child tested Pine Tree, Box-Pine, Pine-Palm, Pine-Rose, or Contra-Rose. These trees are all in the Pine Tree family. Also read chapter 9 if your child is not a "pure" Pine Tree.

In this chapter:

- Meet Samantha, the natural Pine Tree.
- Develop—how to nurture the nature of a young Pine Tree.
- Direct—what and how to teach a Pine Tree.
- Dialogue—how to speak the Pine Tree dialect.
- Discipline—how to train the Pine Tree way.
- Disciple—shaping the Pine Tree's character for God's purpose.

I am sure all of us become calmer and more relaxed when strolling through a pine forest. The Pine Tree temperament is naturally unruffled and has a calming effect on the rest of us.

The roots of a pine tree are so deeply anchored that you need a huge shovel to uproot even a small seedling. Pine Tree people are the same—strongly rooted, stubborn in a quiet way, and not eager to be transplanted.

Pine trees in a plantation are usually all the same size and shape. Similarly, people with Pine Tree temperaments can blend in with their surroundings and easily escape our attention. They don't advertise themselves, they avoid the spotlight, and they may be perfectly happy to be in the background.

Just as pine trees are seldom found alone and are associated with Christmas, so people with Pine Tree characteristics are attached to their families, loyal to their friends, happy to be with people, and fond of tradition.

MEET SAMANTHA, THE NATURAL PINE TREE

As a baby, Samantha was happy to lie in her crib most of the time. Her mother practically took her out only to change her diapers. She skipped the terrible twos altogether, remaining cooperative and content. Samantha was an angel at age four. She sat still at the table and said thank you and please without being told to, and never demanded what was not on her plate.

But Samantha was sometimes a frustration to her Boxwood mom. She was hard to get going when it was time to bathe, go to bed, get dressed, or go shopping. Talk about stubborn! She claimed she couldn't get into the bath on her own or put on her own clothes; she refused to even try to put away her books and toys. "I'm too small. The puzzle has too many pieces. It will take me all day and all night. The Legos hurt me when I pick them up. Mommy must do it." Shopping made her tired. "Carry me!" was her typical plea.

As long as a chore was not too exhausting and Mom or Dad offered to help, it pleased her to do what was expected. If the command came fast and had to be obeyed immediately, the little princess deflated like a punctured jumping castle. The helpless bundle would stare at her parents with an expression of disbelief! How could they make such unreasonable demands?

In elementary school the teacher remarked that Samantha was sweet but usually last to finish her work. She drifted and dreamed in class. When students were asked to participate, she broke eye contact and tried to be invisible to avoid speaking in front of the class. On the playground, she kept to one best friend or simply watched the other kids play. She felt sorry for the kids who had no friends but wasn't bold enough to befriend them herself.

As she headed into her teens, she was often so passive and listless that her parents felt the need to take her pulse every now and then to make sure she was still alive ... Okay, I'm exaggerating! But she showed little interest in anything besides art and novels. She was clearly not going to become a competitive team sports player! Her mom regularly had to resist the temptation to complete the school assignments Samantha procrastinated and didn't finish on time.

People likely said some of these things about her:

- "You are as steady as a rock."
- "You don't wear your heart on your sleeve."
- "Even a bomb threat can't get you moving."
- "With you, what you see is what you get."
- "Don't you ever get excited?"

DEVELOP — HOW TO NURTURE THE NATURE OF A YOUNG PINE TREE

In your child's Tall Trees Kids Profile Report, these tailor-made needs
will be listed as the Pine Tree's "Fertilizer."

1. Harmony among family members: Tension and conflict, such
as those caused by divorce, fights, or financial pressure, paralyze
Pine Trees. They should be shielded from such problems and the
resulting emotions. Reassure them that the problems or unhappiness
will eventually pass. Even schoolwork or performance on the sports
field suffers when they lack the security of harmonious relationships
at home.

2. Traditions, stability, and basic things that remain constant:
Pine Trees enjoy holidays celebrated at the same place every year and
their own seats at the table and in the car. Moving house—or even
moving to a different room!—should be approached with care and
advance notice. Pine Trees are slow to make new friends and take a
long time to put down new roots. Make sure you have many family
traditions and special times together.

When we remodeled our previous home, we knocked out a wall
between the playroom and the living room to create one large living
space. Mindful of our daughter's resistance to change, we had her
draw on the walls before knocking them out, to turn it into a positive

experience. Our Pine Tree sat weeping in the rubble nevertheless, crying, "My playroooom!"

3. A group to belong to: Pine Trees are often wallflowers and spectators, and they create the impression that they don't have social needs. They are, however, sensitive to rejection by their peers and family. They don't have to be the center of attention—in fact, they seldom enjoy the spotlight—but they do want to be invited and need to belong. Pine Trees can derive pleasure from other people's joy without sharing in the action themselves.

Remember that the family is the best and first circle to feel a part of.

4. Encouragement without pressure and criticism: Pine Trees may not show it, but they are sensitive to criticism. They simply stop trying when they repeatedly get the impression that somebody is not satisfied. Try to walk beside them all the way with loving support and understanding. Deal with their failures as calmly as you can so they can get up and try again.

Readiness is one of the things that plays a big part in the courage of Pine Trees. Anyone who has ever tried to teach Pine Trees to dive into a pool will know that they simply aren't ready until they are ready! If your Pine Tree refuses to accept a challenge, step back and allow him space and time. He will know by himself when the right moment has come to jump into the pool.

> *If failure isn't acceptable, trial and error are thrown out*
> *as a learning strategy and kids resort to compliance, docile*
> *repetition, and playing it safe. What could be more boring*
> *and less challenging than that? There's got to be another way.*
> Jim Hancock, *Raising Adults*

5. Lots of time with parents: Pine Trees talk less than other children, have few demands, and don't easily let us into their hearts. Consequently, they are easily overlooked. They need their own people, especially their parents, more than they let on, and they will trust someone with their secrets and feelings only if that person willingly spends time with them and shows sincere interest.

These are not children we can put to bed in two minutes with a hug and a kiss. They need us to make time to go and sit or lie quietly with them. Our body language and tone of voice should be relaxed so as to convey the message clearly: "Here I am now. I enjoy spending time with you. Talk to me if you want to. Just sit quietly next to me if you like—no pressure, no expectations."

6. Enough time to process and respond: Pine Trees think and act carefully and slowly. They are tranquil souls who respond cautiously to requests and instructions. Patience is the key! We can figuratively post a sign that says "Decisions ahead" to warn them of an upcoming choice: "Think about what you would like to do for your birthday next month, then we can discuss it over dinner sometime next week."

They are not great at obeying immediately upon the first request. To my shame, I have to admit that my sweet Pine Tree daughter got some undeserved spankings as a two- and three-year-old for obeying too slowly to my liking. I didn't realize that slowness is not the same as unwillingness. What I now understand is that every Pine Tree hears commands and requests with an unspoken coda—"please obey at your earliest convenience"—and, of course, it will be convenient a little later! They want to think, and then, as my dear friend from the

Deep South says, they want to fix on getting ready to maybe start on moseying out to do it.

7. Time to relax and just do nothing: Even as babies, Pine Trees are calmer than other saplings and usually sleep more. They simply need a lot of rest and leisure time.

They are often so passive that we fear they might grow moss if they stayed in one place any longer, especially when they are teenagers! (Help your Pine Trees make good choices if you see that all their relaxation takes place in front of screens.)

8. Opportunities to discover themselves: Most Pine Trees will have one passion in life and, consequently, will not get excited about many other things. We would be wise not to apply too much pressure but instead expose our Pine Trees to as many options as possible until we find something that ignites their passion. Beware of forcing your own interests on them. The more pressure we exert, the more difficult it is for a Pine Tree to explore activities and find their true interests.

Pine Trees can see from the sidelines whether they will enjoy something. They have a good idea of what they can and can't do. That is why they will flatly refuse to do certain things, even to try just once. Respect this.

Once they find their "one thing," they need our support in it. Pine Trees who are denied their one passion can be broken for life. When we disregard their interests, we make them feel lonely and worthless. Feeling like nobody understands them may even put them at risk of contemplating suicide. According to a counselor friend of mine, who has extensive experience with suicidal teens, it is a critical issue for Pine Trees in particular to have their father's support in pursuing their one passion.

9. Time to make peace after conflict: Pine Trees are more afraid of conflict than anything else (criticism and having to make choices under pressure are also high on the list). After every incident, make sure they know the conflict is over. If we have to scold them or punish them, they need to hear in so many words afterward that we aren't angry anymore and that everything is right again.

10. Role models with integrity: Pine Trees aren't easily impressed, nor do they get carried away. However, there is one exception. When a Pine Tree meets a role model who has integrity, honesty, and steadfastness, that person will attract a Pine Tree like a magnet and can get her motivated and moving (two tough challenges with some Pines). The young Pine Tree will know this person is "nice" only when what she is sensing is genuineness and warmth. Such a person may be a piano teacher or a friend's mom (which could make us feel second rate). Pine Trees will idealize and follow such a person while searching for their own place to "be nice." Of course, most parents wish to fulfill this mentorship role. If, however, our Pine Trees choose mentors outside of our homes, this is neither unusual nor an accusation against us. It is just a "safer" choice for them.

11. Something or someone to nurture: Most Pine Trees are natural caregivers. They should at least have potted plants or pets or a hobby that allows them to hone this talent, such as cooking. This also gives them an opportunity to acquire a sense of responsibility. When they are old enough, they should be encouraged to help take care of the elderly, the sick, or the poor. They are also patient and

caring helpers for the mom and the babysitter, and can make great babysitters themselves when they reach the appropriate age.

DIRECT — WHAT AND HOW TO TEACH A PINE TREE

Nothing makes one quite as productive as the last minute.
Author unknown

Our Pine Trees need to learn:

1. To overcome laziness and stop putting off tasks: Pine Trees sometimes need a gentle nudge when they don't do their fair share. Explain to them how other people feel when someone in the group doesn't pull his weight. A Pine Tree is a lot like a wind-up toy— willing and able to move, but not without someone else turning the key. My Pine Tree husband jokingly defends this trait, claiming Pine Trees just "don't want to peak too soon!"

Pine Trees often see the task ahead as daunting. We can teach them that the sooner they start, the sooner they'll finish. It helps to allocate a time to each part of the chore, thereby ensuring the task doesn't spoil their whole day as they fear it might.

Work expands to fill the time available for its completion.
Cyril Northcote Parkinson, *Parkinson's Law*

2. To motivate themselves: When our Pine Trees stop short of a task, we have to help them find reasons to complete the tasks they start. We may openly ask questions such as, "What will it take to

motivate you to finish clearing the table? What will it cost [not in terms of money] to get you to wake up on time?"

Initially, we may need to help a young child think of ideas. Start off with basic things so that the rewards don't get out of hand! If this kind of motivation doesn't sound educational to you, remember that we also reward ourselves with all kinds of treats after we file our tax returns, go to the dentist or gynecologist, sort out the pantry, or finally repair the leaking roof.

Teach your Pine Tree to keep in mind the opportunities available after the chore: "Remember, the sooner you have a bath, the sooner you can get on with your computer game."

3. To put emotions and needs into words: The emotional vocabulary of Pine Trees is typically limited: "I feel good. I don't feel so good. I feel happy, sad, afraid, or angry," and their favorite, "I'm fine." We can teach our Pine Trees to value their feelings and to put them into words more accurately by describing their emotions for them: "I see that you are unhappy. You must have felt embarrassed when your friend let out your secret in class. It makes us feel small to be humiliated like that in front of everyone."

Sometimes we also need to take our Pine Trees to the "shop" by asking key questions about their needs, because when we ask a Pine Tree, "Do you need anything?" we will most likely hear, "Not really," or, "Nothing I can think of at the moment." We can help them decide by asking instead, "Is there anyone you would like to visit?" or, "Can you remind me what games you really enjoy?"

4. To deal assertively with conflict: Pine Trees tend to run away from fights without defending themselves. They're not usually asser-tive, and they tend to keep quiet when unpleasant things happen to

them. This is because they fear conflict and lack conflict-resolution skills. We need to teach them the value of conflict. For instance, we sometimes have to take a stand against something or somebody so that something good can happen. Lightbulbs make light because the wire inside "fights" the electricity that runs through it. Read Pine Trees stories of activists and social reformers such as Martin Luther King Jr. and Nelson Mandela, who was a Pine Tree fighter without whom the world would have less peace today!

Pine Trees are easily bullied because bullies know they probably won't fight back. They cry more easily than Rose Bushes and usually, like Boxwoods, don't have a huge circle of friends, which makes them easy targets. They don't talk much, so it is unlikely that they will tell anyone that they are being bullied.

If you find out that your Pine Tree is a victim of bullying, teach your child to be assertive in the following ways:

- Choose to befriend people who will help defend you against the bully—a teacher, your friends, or other victims who are too scared to stand up to the bully alone.
- Always stand up straight and look the bully in the eye.
- Don't cry or run away if you can help it. This gives the bully a reason to choose you as a victim again.
- Clearly tell the bully what behavior you don't like and won't allow: "You are not allowed to steal my snack money. Stop doing it. I won't cry anymore, and I won't run away again either. I will make

sure you get in trouble for this." (Your Pine Tree
will need to rehearse this!)

- Always tell someone, until something is done
  about the bully. Don't ever feel guilty. A tattletale
  complains over silly little things to get others into
  trouble. Bullying is not silly—it is serious. You
  can get help for yourself and the bully when you
  tell someone!

- If nothing else works, scream "No!" loudly and
  angrily. It's better than crying because this kind
  of scream usually attracts the assistance of the
  right people and focuses the attention on the
  victim instead of the bully. He won't like this
  at all, and it might make him think twice in the
  future.

5. To say what they think without mincing words: Pine
Trees are masters at hinting. When my daughter wanted to know
whether I had bought her any treats, it usually took about five
minutes because she beat around the bush. "Mom, I see you've
already packed all the cold stuff in the fridge, so there's only stuff
for the bathroom or grocery cupboard in the other bags. I can't
see what's in them—the shelf is too high. Do you mind if I peek?
I will help you put them away, except if there is perhaps a small
secret or surprise in there"—I still don't take the bait!—"or is there
something that my brother and I shouldn't see? Something that
isn't very healthy? Maybe something that shouldn't be eaten before
dinner?"

Sometimes this long introduction is amusing, but other times it makes me impatient. She has to learn that it is safe to say, "Mom, do you have candy in those bags that I may eat now?"

6. To respect others by being on time: Because Pine Trees have respect for other people's feelings—often more so than Rose Bushes and Palm Trees do—they can be taught to understand how important punctuality is for their relationships with others. Being late conveys a message of disregard, apathy, or poor self-control and can cause people to have negative feelings about you.

To teach them time management, we need to give our Pine Trees alarm clocks and watches from an early age and coach them to use these tools.

7. To make choices and follow through with action: Pine Trees are afraid of choices because of the finality of a decision. They tend to wonder if they could have made a better choice—perhaps their choice will upset someone or cause problems down the line. They are naturally slow at making decisions, and sometimes this prevents them from making a decision altogether. When we judge them or accuse them of making wrong choices, it makes them only more cautious in the future.

When Pine Trees have made a decision, however, encourage them to start executing the plan immediately.

Our Pine Trees learn best:

- by observing how others do it
- when there is space and time for mistakes and second chances
- by completing a task with the help of someone else

- when we focus on the process rather than the end results
- when a huge task is divided into realistic smaller steps
- when they have a good relationship with all the people in the situation
- when the parent is willing to support without criticizing
- when they don't have to take risks in front of other people
- when they can work alone if they prefer to
- from a role model whom they trust completely

DIALOGUE — HOW TO SPEAK THE PINE TREE DIALECT

How does God speak to Pine Trees?

> *The LORD had said to Abram, "Go from your country, your people and your father's household to the land I will show you. I will make you into a great nation, and I will bless you; I will make your name great, and you will be a blessing. I will bless those who bless you, and whoever curses you I will curse; and all peoples on earth will be blessed through you."*
>
> Genesis 12:1–3 NIV

> *When Abram was ninety-nine years old, the LORD appeared to him and said, "I am God Almighty; walk before me faithfully and be blameless. Then I will make my covenant between me and you and*

will greatly increase your numbers." Abram fell facedown, and God said to him, "As for me, this is my covenant with you: You will be the father of many nations. No longer will you be called Abram; your name will be Abraham, for I have made you a father of many nations. I will make you very fruitful; I will make nations of you, and kings will come from you. I will establish my covenant as an everlasting covenant between me and you and your descendants after you for the generations to come, to be your God and the God of your descendants after you. The whole land of Canaan, where you now reside as a foreigner, I will give as an everlasting possession to you and your descendants after you; and I will be their God."

Genesis 17:1–8 NIV

The Lord talks to Abraham from a relationship perspective, using words like *father, family, descendants,* and *nation* because this appeals to Abraham's temperament (Genesis 12:2; 15:4–6, 13; 17:1–8). It's important for a Pine Tree to belong to a family or a group.

Because the Lord knows how hard it is for a Pine Tree to simply uproot and move away from everything and everyone he knows, the Lord immediately gives Abraham a new vision—a new horizon (Genesis 12:1–3).

The Lord gives Abraham the bottom line with few details. Each time God speaks to Abraham, it is with basically the same message—descendants, a promised land, and an eternal covenant (Genesis 12–18). Pine Trees don't need a lot of details!

The Lord speaks to Abraham about his future and about people, not tasks. God knows that security and family are the things that resonate with Pine Trees; He made them that way, after all.

The Lord negotiates rationally and honestly with Abraham about the destruction of Sodom and Gomorrah—there is no emotional content in the conversation despite the intensely devastating thing that is about to happen (Genesis 18:17–32).

The Lord gives promises, knowing that a Pine Tree with his patient nature will hold on to them. God gives Abraham the security every Pine Tree wants by repeatedly talking about the eternal covenant and the many descendants who would continue enjoying its blessing long after Abraham's death (Genesis 17:7, 13, 19).

How should we talk to our Pine Trees?

When we want our Pine Trees to listen attentively instead of switching off while we are speaking, the following guidelines may help:

Stand, sit, or lie next to your child and make sure your whole body and face is relaxed and friendly before you start talking.

Talk slowly and calmly and look your child in the eye. If your Pine Tree enjoys physical contact, touch her while speaking to her.

Refrain from using criticism as a means to spur your Pine Tree on—it has the opposite effect. My Pine Tree husband calls them "wet wood" because "all you get when you try to light a fire under them is smoke in your eyes!" Avoid all insulting, aggressive, sarcastic, and derogatory words. Stick to the facts.

Communicate from within the relationship. Give "us messages" rather than "you messages" or "I messages." For example, say "Why don't we try once more to solve this math problem?" rather than "You'll have to try again. Don't be a quitter."

Simplify the choices you expect your Pine Tree to make, and model confident decision making. Pine Trees find security in your self-assurance. They will accept your decisions more easily if they have a trusting relationship with you.

When you shout, Pine Trees tune out. They distance themselves from anyone they feel doesn't deserve their respect. Hysterical parents definitely fall into this category. Such parents may end up facing a Pine Tree child with a message on his forehead reading "You are no longer subscribed to this channel."

> *Trying to control children by screaming is as utterly*
> *futile as trying to steer a car by honking the horn.*
> Dr. James Dobson, *The Complete Family and Marriage Home Reference Guide*

Steer clear of unnecessary questions. Pine Trees are threatened by what they perceive as cross-examinations. It's better to make statements and wait for them to agree, to disagree, or to ask for more information.

When you have to ask serious questions, make a special effort to introduce the topic gently, and allow time for their reactions.

Keep "lectures" short and sweet. Pine Trees listen for the bottom line and can get lost in too many details.

Talk about the future. The Pine Tree's focus is on the long term, or the potential prospects. If, for instance, you explain the principles of table manners, describe how good manners will earn people's respect someday.

How can we listen to our Pine Trees better?

Be patient with your Pine Tree's long-windedness. Once she starts talking, you may be surprised how long she can carry on. If you get impatient, however, it may well be the last deep conversation your child will have with you.

Pine Trees don't get right to the point until they feel safe to do so. Once, my Pine Tree daughter pulled me into such a drawn-out discussion. She had a myriad of questions about the second coming of Jesus. "What if I am in the bath when He comes?" and "When He comes, everyone will see Him, so the earth will have to fold down flat like a map. What if we fall off the edge?" I was in a hurry because I had writing deadlines to meet, and finally, her pressing question came out: "If Jesus doesn't look like the pictures in the children's Bible, how will we know that it's really Him?" I have a tendency to cross the line with sarcastic humor, and I thought of saying, "Just watch the face of our atheist neighbor. If he looks freaked out, it's Jesus." That would have spoiled what was about to be one of the most precious moments ever with my Pine Tree daughter. Before I could say this foolish thing, she said, "Wait! I know! My spirit will know that it's Jesus and my spirit will tell me to run, run, run!" I asked why she would run, assuming she would be running away. "I will run into His arms because He will be really happy to see me!"

Don't interrupt Pine Trees. Their pauses are long because they are processing and thinking before they speak. Give them time. If they have fast-talking Palm Tree and Rose Bush siblings, create ways for them to get a word in.

Enjoy their dry sense of humor. This is one of their most endearing characteristics.

If your Pine Tree is exceptionally shy, don't force him to talk in front of an audience. Respect the courage it takes for him to do this. Refrain from criticizing when he gets stage fright or becomes shy. Let's be realistic—very few Pine Trees are going to need those public-speaking classes their parents bully them into. God has an offstage place for most of them to speak to small groups or individuals one on one. There are times when Pine Trees simply either won't talk or can't talk—please respect that.

Pine Trees tend to manipulate with silence because words are power. One can't force open the oyster and expect a pearl to roll out. Wait for it to open by itself. Yet, insist that they do deal with the issue eventually.

Because Pine Trees are not frequently talkative, we have to "listen" to more than their words. Note their body language, facial expressions, sleeping and eating patterns, habits, and schoolwork to make sure all is well.

The most important thing in communication is to hear what is not said.

Peter F. Drucker, *Classic Drucker*

In summary:

- Set an example.
- Give the instruction in parts.
- Offer help and support.
- Give your time and attention.
- Appreciate the willing heart.

DISCIPLINE — HOW TO TRAIN THE PINE TREE WAY

Each tree type has its own pruning and watering needs. These approaches work the best with Pine Trees:

1. Strategies and structure: Pine trees growing from the ground don't need pruning. At most they need a prop when they are planted in a windy spot. However, even that isn't necessary if they're planted among other pines. Pine Tree children are the same. They only need a prop or scaffolding sometimes, and having powerful models in their homes or social circles is often enough to help them grow properly.

The props they occasionally need are strategies and structure. Pine Trees can be dreamy and distractible; therefore, a watch on the arm is not enough. Use a timer or alarm clock to help them manage their time. For instance, a clock can be set for five minutes after they get up in the morning to prompt them to get dressed. Then you might set it for five minutes later to draw their attention to brush their hair and teeth, and so on.

2. Sweat and discomfort: Being such experts on ease, young Pine Trees tend to avoid physically hard work. Consequences for misbehavior that require extra effort and time away from their favorite bed, chair, or carpet will definitely drive the point home. Room-temperature drinking water for the boy who leaves food out of the fridge, or no bubble baths for the girl who leaves the bathroom in shambles, for example.

3. A personal message: Pine Trees want to know that things between them and other people are fine. They are the tree type with the most active "social conscience." It's effective to tell them how

their behavior affects you and others. They'll feel rewarded when you encourage good behavior by explaining the effect it has on you: "When you tidy your room on your own, it really helps me because then I don't need to think of all the tasks that need doing. Now we can have a relaxed chat and a Bible story before bedtime instead."

Pine Trees experience a lot of what is happening around them as too quick, too loud, too busy, and overwhelming; therefore, they tend to shut down or tune out many things. When we tell them something positive in that same busy way, they probably don't hear that either. If we truly want to encourage and inspire them, we may need to sit with them calmly, or even lie down with them, and say something simple and sincere, such as, "You're doing much better with being on time for activities. I enjoy not having to rush you."

4. Stern or calm words (including tone of voice and facial expressions): Pine Trees won't usually burst into tears as easily as Boxwoods (although the babies will), but our words have an impact on them because they too are sensitive. They don't like seeing us angry or upset, so they often need no more than a raised eyebrow or a single word to get them back on the straight and narrow. This "look" and those "words" ought to be used with care. The look doesn't have to kill, and the words shouldn't threaten, humiliate, or attack. A simple "We don't sit on a table" is enough.

5. Rational conversations: Unlike Palm Trees, Pine Trees can keep quiet for a long time and listen to reason. They also don't react as emotionally to correction as Boxwoods tend to. They don't get as angry as Rose Bushes either. Sometimes a factual and private conversation about the wrong that was done and what they need to do next time is all that's needed.

6. Rest and relaxation: Relaxation is precious for Pine Trees. Use this as a reward for good behavior. Take care that they don't spend too much time in front of screens (television and computer). Help them from a young age to discover healthier, restful recreational possibilities, such as reading, nature walks, craft work, playing a musical instrument, bird watching, photography, or music appreciation.

7. Time spent with you as a reward: Individual time with their parents is one of the best incentives for Pine Trees. It doesn't have to be exciting—they'll likely prefer something quiet and relaxed. It can be as simple as cuddling up next to your reading Pine Tree with your own book as soon as all the homework is done.

A CULTIVATION PLAN FOR PINE TREES

Pine Trees—like Boxwoods—don't usually misbehave in the traditional sense of the word. Parents seldom complain about what they have done; more often we complain about what they don't want to do! (A consolation—they rarely complain about us.) Usually they are a pleasure to be around until we demand something strenuous from them; they seem to have a law against sweating.

A lot of our energy will be invested in the difficult tasks of teaching our Pine Trees responsibility, reliability, and good work ethics. This will not happen overnight—it will be the result of years of patient accompaniment and modeling.

Pine Trees are gentle children who put good relationships first. We can simplify the task of disciplining them greatly by showing love and interest, and giving them time and individual attention. Pine Trees who have enough of these things seldom feel the need to make trouble. They want to be obedient for the sake of a good relationship because their security depends on it. A good relationship predicts cooperation; a bad relationship predicts trouble. Rigid disciplining techniques don't work with Pine Trees. They shy away from forceful authority figures. We get better results when we use less drastic measures to train them and guide them patiently by helping them think of plans that work for them.

> *Punishment teaches a child to avoid a behavior; excessive punishment teaches a child to avoid the punisher.*
> Ron Morrish, *Secrets of Discipline for Parents and Teachers*

The following plan to change behavior can be used effectively with Pine Trees. Begin by making three lists in the following table of things you want to work on.

To Do Less	To Do More Often	Doing Great!

What does my Pine Tree do too often or incorrectly?

For example: She watches too much television, reads secretly at night and then oversleeps, is late getting to school, spends too much time on social media, avoids making decisions even when she has plenty of time to weigh her options, occupies the bathroom for an hour, and eats too many sweets.

What does my Pine Tree do too infrequently or not at all?

Your list may include the following: He doesn't do his chores regularly, doesn't tidy up without being told, procrastinates when he should study for tests, doesn't offer to help in the house, doesn't greet people by name, and doesn't hand in school assignments on time.

What does my Pine Tree do right or often enough?

You may observe the following: She carries out orders in a friendly manner, enjoys helping in the kitchen, goes to bed without moaning, and spends her allowance discerningly. Focusing on this list of good behaviors will prevent a negative focus in discipline. It will also prevent you from becoming discouraged when other forms of good behavior prove hard to teach.

Now rank each type of behavior according to how urgently you need to attend to it. Mark the highest priority with a 1, and so forth.

Choose only one thing at a time from each list.

Ensure that your spouse, other family members, teachers, and caregivers are aware of your goals and willing to cooperate in setting consistent expectations, rules, consequences, and rewards. For example, everybody should maintain the same rules for watching television; otherwise, your Pine Tree won't learn that certain recreational habits can be harmful.

Decide on a realistic time frame for each goal, and make sure you time the training well. Pine Trees are like photocopiers that can take a while to warm up before they work well. If you can see that you haven't made any progress in a week, abandon the plan and try something else. If necessary, return to the first plan in a month or two. It may not be a good idea to practice waking up on time during the holidays, but the holidays may be the perfect time to work on healthy recreational habits. As soon as one of these objectives is met, move on to number 2 on the list of priorities in the same column, so as never to have more than three challenges simultaneously demanding your attention.

Think about the behavior in the first column. Why does your Pine Tree do it? Which rewards does it have? How can you ensure in a justified, meaningful way that the behavior has negative consequences? With which behavior should your Pine Tree replace it? How can you reward the required behavior once your child starts behaving well?

Take, for example, the Pine Tree who watches too much television. A scolding or spanking won't be necessary—better structure will yield the desired result. Pine Trees complain that there's nothing else for them to do, and while they expect us to come up with ideas, they rarely like what we suggest!

You could decide on a total number of hours per day or week that they may spend in front of the television. Second, sit down with your child and make a list of alternatives, such as reading, cycling, inviting a friend over, walking to the mall (for older kids in a safe neighborhood), putting together a puzzle, writing a letter or making a phone call to a relative, doing crafts, gardening, or playing with a pet. It is important that these alternatives be your child's ideas. Make suggestions, but don't add them to the list without your Pine Tree's agreement. Put up the list in your child's room or next to the

television set so he can see it when he sits down in front of the tube
out of habit. If he sticks to the time limits, allow him bonus time over
weekends. All hours that are "stolen" will unfortunately be deducted
from screen time during the next day or week.

A Pine Tree who oversleeps can simply be expected to go to bed
earlier proportionate to the time she overslept. If she got up at seven
thirty instead of seven, and missed the school bus, she could be sent
to bed at eight instead of eight thirty. Because time management is
often such a challenge for Pine Trees, they need a watch and an alarm
clock in their room. Reward them when they are on time by increasing their relaxation time and giving recognition for the fact that they
are becoming more reliable and punctual.

Think about the behavior on the second list. Why doesn't my
child do what I want her to do? Does my Pine Tree really know
what I expect? Is the behavior I expect realistic given my child's age
and abilities? How can I help my child through the process? Does
she simply forget to do what is required? If so, how can I help her
remember?

Here we can use the example of a ten-year-old who doesn't want
to study for tests. Start by finding out what time of day she is most
alert and industrious. Your Pine Tree will probably want to relax
after school before she can start studying. Maybe she should also be
allowed to study after dinner, or she may like getting up earlier to
study. By helping her find her best study time, you do her a favor that
will reap benefits in the future.

Second, she has to have clear targets. It works best when she
decides for herself which marks she wants to achieve. If you know she
can achieve 80 percent if she exerts herself, but she is quite content

with 65 percent, you might be tempted to pressure her into chasing your standards rather than her own. She won't have your willpower all her life. Let her practice using her own. Let her write down these targets and put them up by her desk. Reward her with study-free days or a movie for hard work, not for specific marks or grades.

Think about the behavior on the third list, and decide how you're going to reward it. There are few encouragements besides your approval and increased comfort that work with Pine Trees because "pure" Pine Trees are unlikely to respond to reward charts or money. If your child doesn't eat enough healthy food to allow for treats as a reward, express your appreciation in words and give special quality time as a reward.

Make sure your child doesn't feel like you want to change her or have high expectations for her to meet, but rather that you want to support her to meet her own expectations. Therefore, reward character and attitude at least as often as you celebrate achievement.

DISCIPLE — SHAPING THE PINE TREE'S CHARACTER FOR GOD'S PURPOSE

Discipling a Pine Tree's heart is a worthwhile journey with many aspects of maturity unfolding rather slowly. Pine Trees are sometimes late bloomers even with spiritual things; although, their contented and easygoing temperament may make them seem wise for their years. When they grow into their sense of purpose, they become the gentle counselors, faithful friends, patient pastors, loving caregivers for the sick and struggling, wise teachers, and loyal assistants to the front-runners. They are servant leadership personified.

Your Pine Tree may not express all the spiritual treasures you have put in him, and you may make the same mistake I made with my Pine Tree daughter when she was around eleven. She was not an eager Bible student like I was at her age, and she rarely spoke spontaneously about spiritual matters. I tried to spur her on, but in all the wrong ways, one day saying, "Your Bible has been in that same spot for weeks. Do you ever read it?" She said, "I don't read it that often, Mom, but each night in my bed I think about God and about how amazing He is, and then I make up new songs for Him in my heart." I learned that with Pine Trees there is always much more going on than meets the eye.

Help them:

1. To take responsibility for their own future and happiness: Pine Trees can sometimes sit and wait for life to happen, and when they don't like what happens, they become morbid. They easily feel that life owes them something and then take on a victim mentality. Pine Trees need to learn that merely "being there" does not entitle them to anything. If they want to achieve success, they will have to work hard for it. They can't wait for God to make good things happen for them without actively walking through the doors He opens. You teach them this by stepping down from your roles as enabler and rescuer.

At risk of being obvious, how surprised should we be when someone raised without a sense of responsibility, without an appreciation for cause and effect, acts irresponsibly and causes regrettable effects? What are we supposed to do about it, you and me? We feel sad and guilty for raising children, when the assignment was to raise adults.

Jim Hancock, *Raising Adults*

2. To take risks, embrace change, and try new things: We should encourage them to do this without pressuring them. This means accepting all our children's attempts, even when they fail. If they ever get the sense that we may reject them or be disappointed by their failure, they won't take risks again. Make sure they are secure in your unconditional love. Start small with encouraging your Pine Tree to order something other than the usual chicken tenders and fries, and work your way toward even greater risks!

3. To stand or fall by their principles: Our Pine Trees place such value on peace that they will sometimes take part in activities under peer pressure just to keep the peace, even if it goes against their values. They are usually innocent and naive, as if they didn't realize that anything was wrong. I once had a conversation with a Pine Tree criminal serving a life sentence. When I asked him about the biggest mistake of his life, he answered without hesitation, "Hanging out with the wrong friends since childhood."

Pine Trees won't conform to everyone's expectations if we teach them from an early age that the most important acceptance is that of the Lord. We need only be acceptable to Him. And that we are, thanks to grace and Jesus's redemptive work on our behalf. Second, they have to accept themselves—something they will be able to do only if they live according to firm principles. Third, the acceptance that comes from people is least important. Those who accept us only when we agree with them are not giving us true acceptance.

4. To give and to share: The need for personal space and privacy includes a Pine Tree's possessions. They can become uncharacteristically angry when someone touches their belongings. Of all the tree types, they have the most difficulty learning to give and share. Accept

that they will likely have one or two treasured toys, garments, or possessions that are more or less "holy" to them. We shouldn't force them to share these items or to give them away. They do, however, need to learn to give and share in other ways:

- Let them eat something, such as popcorn or chips, from the same container as other children. If we always give each child his own bowl, we encourage selfishness.
- Play games where everyone has to take turns, because the principle is the same as sharing.
- Let the children identify toys they are willing to share before other children come over to play.
- If your child's school allows it, pack extra food in his lunch box to give away.
- Let your children serve other people and then help themselves last so they can learn that it is not the end of the world to be last.
- Start a family tradition of giving away (undamaged and clean) clothes, toys, books, videos, and such every season.

5. To become involved and take the lead when necessary: Pine Trees avoid opportunities to lead because they may think leadership means constantly being in conflict or in the limelight. Teach them that different types of leadership are required in different situations. Explain your Pine Tree's unique leadership style to her, namely that she can see the bigger picture and get people to cooperate, she can

stay calm, and she can deter the little things from blinding her. Encourage her to get involved in that way when she has something valuable to contribute. Bringing snacks for everyone is leadership too. Remind her how often Jesus simply sat and ate with people, and their lives were never the same!

LET'S GET PRACTICAL

Because Pine Trees open their hearts only to those who really show an interest in them and spend time with them, we'll reap relational benefits when we set aside special time and make an effort to get to know our Pine Tree children. Why don't we already do this? Mark the reasons that are applicable to you and your child below. Pray about each one, and write down what you can do to change it. Talk to other parents if you need advice.

- I don't know what to say to my Pine Tree; therefore, I choose not to spend time alone with him or her.
- I have so much work that I really don't have time for my Pine Tree during the week.
- My other children are so demanding that there isn't any time left for my Pine Tree. My Pine Tree doesn't insist on attention.
- I don't know my Pine Tree well enough to know where to start.
- My Pine Tree chooses to talk to my spouse rather than to me.

- I am home only on weekends, and I have a right to relax and do what I want then; I don't have the strength to sit around with my Pine Tree as well.
- My Pine Tree doesn't like me. I don't think he or she wants to spend any time with me.

Most of our excuses for spending too little time with our children are based on one of two sad realities: we don't realize how satisfying a deeper relationship with our children can be, or we don't realize how much our children need us. These misconceptions can be reversed when we make an effort to get to know our children and when we see the results of spending time with them.

"Interview" your Pine Tree, even if you ask only one question a day for a few weeks in a row, until you can answer all the questions below. If your child tends to clam up when questioned, you can make statements such as: "It seems to me Janet is your favorite friend" or "I often hear that music coming from your room. It must be your favorite. I don't know that band" or "I see you always do your math homework first. I suppose it is your favorite subject." As you can tell, you will first have to observe your child carefully before you can make these statements. Remember not to react critically or be judgmental about the answers.

Who or what is your child's …

- best friend
- favorite music
- favorite school activity
- favorite game or computer game

- favorite television series
- role model
- favorite color
- favorite teacher
- greatest fear
- favorite vacation destination
- favorite book
- favorite Bible verse and Bible character
- favorite restaurant or dish

What angers your child?

What does your child want to study when he or she grows up?

Where would your child want to live someday?

Which school activity does your child enjoy least?

What causes your child to feel pressured?

CHAPTER 8

A WHOLE NURSERY UNDER ONE ROOF

In this chapter:

- How can we discipline fairly when our saplings differ?
- What is fairness?
- How important is equality?
- What do I owe my child?
- When the apple falls far from the tree.
- Palm Tree parents and their saplings.
- Rose Bush parents and their saplings.
- Boxwood Tree parents and their saplings.
- Pine Tree parents and their saplings.
- Trees from the same plantation.

How can we discipline fairly when our saplings differ? It can be very difficult to keep your wits about you when there are different varieties in your nursery! Each will react to a unique set of incentives, and each has his or her own unique needs. Parents often ask me what to do when a Palm Tree and a Boxwood get into trouble together. Should one go and sit in his room while the other one gets a spanking? Is that fair? Which brings us to an important parenting question:

WHAT IS FAIRNESS?

We have to look past the obvious when we punish or reward our children. When children do something wrong together, their roles and motives are seldom identical. Their experiences of the same consequences will also differ. Studies have found that siblings accept their parents treating them differently, provided that the children each regard their own treatment as fair. In fact, they often feel it is unfair to be treated alike. The parents should, however, explain the reasons clearly to their children.[13]

When a two-year-old and an eight-year-old spread manure all over their father's motorcycle, there are various reasons why they ought to be punished differently for the same misbehavior.

Age: The eight-year-old should be punished because she knew what she was doing, while the two-year-old may be excused because she couldn't yet grasp the difference between manure and car polish.

History: If this is the fourth time the eight-year-old has done this, it should be clear that talking doesn't help; therefore, she should be punished more severely this time. The two-year-old can only receive a scolding—a "suspended sentence" if you will—and perhaps her first oral instruction in why she is not allowed to play with the motorcycle.

Abilities: Both will have to clean up, but because the little sister is only two, Dad could help her hold the hose. The older sister may have to sit there for a couple of hours with a toothbrush to remove all the bits from every nook and cranny.

Intentions: The eight-year-old may be angry because she is not allowed to ride on the motorcycle with her dad, so her motive could be revenge. The two-year-old probably thought she was helping her big sister with an important chore. In this case the older child is the only one who should be punished.

Temperament: Suppose the older child is a Pine Tree who rarely openly defies Mom and Dad. She knows she has to accept Dad's decision, but she is really unhappy about it. This mischief is the only way for her to express her anger about not being allowed to ride with him. Discussing the reasons for Dad's decision will work much better than a spanking to ensure that it doesn't happen again. If the younger sister is a busy Palm Tree who can't stand still long enough to listen to reason, she will gain more from a forceful *"No!"* than from a long explanation.

But how do you explain to children why they are being treated differently? This raises a second question:

HOW IMPORTANT IS EQUALITY?

What does the world for which we are preparing our children look like? It isn't a world in which employees receive equal bonuses or promotions. It is a world in which competition means only one winner and many losers. When your wealthy neighbor buys his wife a brand-new car, he doesn't give you a secondhand rust bucket as a consolation prize! This is the life we have to prepare our children for—a life where equality plays a small role. Jesus tells the disillusioning tale of the landlord who pays his workers the same wage, irrespective of the number of hours they worked (Matthew 20:1–16). This reveals that we should not expect to experience equality as we know it in the life hereafter either! Our children should learn to sing "happy birthday to you" and "happy birthday to me" with the same joyfulness. By the way, in my opinion this is one of the keys to raising happy, contented children: do not spoil them with the artificial "equality" of giving every child a present when one sibling has a birthday.

WHAT DO I OWE MY CHILDREN?

The Lord is apparently unfair when punishing and rewarding His children here on earth. David complains that the Lord even treats the disobedient better than the well-behaved ones, and strangers better than His own children (Psalm 74). In Job 27:1–2, Job complains about not being treated fairly, then the Lord reacts to these accusations (Job 38–41, especially 40:1–8). By implication, the Lord is saying, "I decide what is right. Who are you to question My judgment?" Obviously we're not in the same position as God in relation to our children, but we can learn some parenting lessons from this. The Lord takes people on a road to spiritual maturity, and we, in turn, lead our children to adulthood. Each journey is unique. There can never be a fixed set of "fair" parenting actions.

Accept the inevitable: Every child clings to the idea that the world should treat him or her as a special case. Your job as a parent is to pry this fantasy from the child's grip. As you do so, it becomes inevitable that your child will not like many of the decisions you make.

Lyndon Waugh, "Avoid Arguments with Your Kids"

We don't always owe our children an explanation, and we definitely won't always be fair in their opinion. As we can't understand all of God's reasons, but still are expected to trust and obey, our kids need not agree with our motivations. Our "mysterious ways" won't hurt them as long as they know they are loved.

When we get into arguments with our children, we usually lose if we start off with long explanations. We look guilty, as if we are trying to defend our point of view. This affords our children an opportunity to challenge us even more vehemently. The less we say after we have drawn the line, the better. We should only be convinced in our own hearts that we have done what is needed in a situation, and that we have done it in a way that is best for each child.

When parents feel obliged to give several reasons for
every request, children develop "parent deafness."
Heidi Langley, play therapist

The conclusion is that I may indeed treat my children differently. In fact, I have to do this if I hope to give each one what he or she needs most. This applies not only to punishment, of course, but also to love. A Pine Tree will frown embarrassedly if you publicly encourage or praise her too enthusiastically. A wink or smile is enough for her and doesn't cause her embarrassment. A Palm Tree will thrive on praise words like "Good job!" and "Wow, you are a little trouper!" while many Boxwoods appreciate notes and tokens more than spoken words. Rose Bushes' parents get a great response when they "promote" their kids to more responsibility and choices— not a Pine Tree's idea of a reward at all!

WHEN THE APPLE FALLS FAR FROM THE TREE

Temperament differences don't equate temperament clashes when we understand the unique dynamics between our personality and our child's. In each combination of parent and child, our personality shapes theirs and vice versa, and there are situations of "friction," "fire," and "flow" because of our differences. These ideas may help you avoid the first two effectively.

PALM TREE PARENTS AND THEIR SAPLINGS

A Palm Tree parent and a Rose Bush sapling

Don't feel rejected when your Rose Bush shies away from the pampering that comes so naturally to you—remember, it's not personal! It's just temperament and preferences. Use your gift of encouraging words to convey your love in your Rose Bush's love language.

Rose Bushes are annoyed by silliness when there is a task at hand, so be careful with the timing of your jokes.

Your fun-loving, easygoing nature will make it difficult for you to enforce strict rules and discipline. However, Rose Bushes need a firm hand and won't take you seriously or accept your authority unless you follow through with discipline.

Rose Bushes have to see that you mean business; otherwise, they will lose respect for you. Choose a few core rules by which you are willing to stand or fall.

Your temperament is inclined to be too quick to talk. Take time to think about your decisions, and be sure about your reasons when you say no, because a Rose Bush will frequently question you about them.

Beware of empty promises, because Rose Bushes are hard on unreliable people.

Try to stick to the facts, because Rose Bushes are much more rational than emotional.

Palm Tree parents tend to concentrate on appearances, popularity, and achievements but need to notice their child's subtle character flaws as well in order to work more on the heart than the performance.

A Palm Tree parent and a Boxwood sapling

Your biggest challenge will likely be to deal with your Boxwood's negative emotions (sadness, despondency, pessimism, disappointment, and so on). Read the section dealing with this as often as necessary, and resist the temptation to cheer up your Boxwood impatiently.

Learn to listen more and talk less! Your Boxwood needs your understanding more than your advice and optimistic perspective. Rest assured, the more patiently you listen, the sooner your child will cheer up.

You will need to be serious about the important, deep matters in your Boxwood's life and not make light of them. Your humor will find outlets elsewhere.

> *Humor is not a trick, not jokes. Humor is a presence in the world—like grace—and shines on everybody.*
> Garrison Keillor, *A Prairie Home Companion*

It comes naturally to you to amuse people with entertaining stories and your sense of humor. Do not embarrass your self-conscious Boxwoods by discussing their mistakes or behavior with friends.

For the sake of your organized Boxwood, who needs a lot of structure and order, learn to plan and follow a routine. Maybe the other parent should take responsibility for transporting your Boxwood to places where it's important to be on time—like to school!

Try to set targets for the education of your children, because a Boxwood wants to know where everyone is headed. Instead of trying to cheer up your Boxwood when he's disappointed in a grade that was lower than he hoped for, support his own performance targets.

A Palm Tree parent and a Pine Tree sapling

> *For fast-acting relief, try slowing down.*
> Lily Tomlin, *Lily Tomlin: The Search for Signs of Intelligent Life in the Universe*

You may have to discover a calm in you that you didn't know you had. When your Pine Tree talks and moves slowly, you will need to stand still, sit down, talk calmly, and listen attentively even though you find doing so difficult.

Your sense of adventure, love of risk taking, and many interests should not be a standard your Pine Tree must meet, because Pine Trees can't function the way you do—they typically don't have the physical energy or psychological makeup for that!

Take special care to be honest and sincere. When you flatter or praise them with ulterior motives, they see right through it, which makes them feel insecure. Say what you mean and mean what you say.

Beware of being too dramatic or overemotional when discussing important issues with your Pine Trees. Even your volume can raise their anxiety.

Learn to listen with your whole body. Stop everything you are busy with and relax. Turn to face your child. Make eye contact and physical contact (if your child welcomes it). Smile. Wait until your child has stopped talking long enough to ensure that it is your turn to speak.

Your Pine Tree teenagers will not appreciate it if you try to steal the spotlight when their friends come to visit. Keep a low profile. This is one of the most important ways you can convey respect and sensitivity to your Pine Tree teenager.

ROSE BUSH PARENTS AND THEIR SAPLINGS

A Rose Bush parent and a Pine Tree sapling

Remember that a Pine Tree doesn't attach much value to competition. Therefore, don't make too much of winning and losing. Concentrate on the process rather than the outcome, especially when you're dissatisfied with her achievements.

Practice applying less pressure to your Pine Tree. Rushing, criticism, and accusations may come naturally when you are in a hurry or disappointed in your child's behavior, but unfortunately these things can make the Pine Tree feel unloved, unsafe, and unhappy.

Your temperament is so task oriented that it may be difficult for you to just be with your Pine Tree. Don't fall into the trap of thinking that "quick quality time" is enough for these saplings. Sometimes, in order to really make contact, you have to go and lie still (!) next to your child without any agenda.

You're likely to expect immediate, unconditional obedience without back talk. Your Pine Tree can do almost nothing immediately or quickly. Allow a few extra seconds for his response.

Apologize when you are wrong. Withholding apologies wounds any child, but Pine Trees probably most of all. They typically can't demand an apology and won't easily open up their hearts to you unless you learn to say you are sorry. They tend to shut a door between you and them that can only be opened from their side.

Beware of doing everything for your Pine Tree and jumping each time she can't react as quickly as you would like. This tendency can turn your Pine Tree into a helpless dependent.

If you haven't learned to find an appropriate outlet for your stress outside of your home (a Rose Bush necessity), your Pine Tree will probably suffer most. Conflict is their greatest fear. Therefore, deal with it in private and swiftly, if possible.

If I say, "Stop nagging! You kids are killing me!" I should at least have the decency to die the next time one of them nags me.
Jim Hancock, *Raising Adults*

A Rose Bush parent and a Palm Tree sapling

Unfortunately, it is not in your nature to like laid-back party people; therefore, it may be hard for you to accept that your Palm Tree can't always keep tasks and targets in mind. Allow plenty of space for play and socializing.

Be careful not to ignore your Palm Tree's need for attention. If you acknowledge his cute voice mimicry while he tells you a story, he may not need to add so many untrue details and wild movements to impress you!

Try to keep in mind that kids are kids. One day you'll realize it was funny when your child said to grown-up company, "I can burp in three syllables already, just like Shrek."

You probably believe that your way is the most effective way. Your Palm Tree is wired to explore alternative ways. Allow for this, as long as the task can still be completed.

> *Discoveries are often made by not following instructions,*
> *by going off the main road, by trying the untried.*
> Frank Tyger, *Forbes Business Quotations*

Your Palm Tree will stay a child in the core of her being for a long time. You may have too little inner child left to appreciate this. Don't expect too much too soon from your Palm Tree, and don't give up. Your "all-grown-up-ness" is exhausting to her—allow for laughter.

You may tend to show little physical affection. Your Palm Tree could wither without this or venture into a physical relationship to fulfill this need. There is only a tiny part nurse and Santa Claus in a typical Rose Bush. These need to grow so that you can address the saplings' great demand for loving care and touch. My husband often helps me curb my Rose Bush tendencies. Once, when I stormed into a situation where our Palm Tree kid got hurt, my husband whispered, "Less Hitler; more Florence Nightingale!"

A Rose Bush parent and a Boxwood sapling

Your biggest challenge may be your possible insensitivity toward emotions. You are at risk of missing it when your Boxwood needs you in this regard unless you make a point of looking for signs of emotional needs.

If you ever trample your Boxwood's emotions, you must do something that is likely difficult for you—ask for forgiveness. Boxwoods don't easily forget; you can't simply hope time will heal the wounds. Your misstep is in the memory bank.

Your Boxwood needs private space where you can't just barge in, and Rose Bush parents don't always regard a closed door as a boundary. Teenagers especially need you to respect their privacy, except when your gut tells you there is something dangerous your child is hiding from you.

You are both task oriented, and your Boxwood usually feels safe under your firm wing. However, you will clash if each wants to do things his or her own way. Agree on the goal; make peace with his method.

Give your Boxwood straight answers and clear instructions. Boxwoods like guidelines, but not someone breathing down their necks—just like you! Give them space rather than keeping them on a short leash. If your Boxwood lacks stamina or optimism, he needs support rather than pressure.

Boxwoods can be guilt magnets. Never blame them for your bad days because they will actually believe they are at fault.

> *The truth is that our children never anger us; they*
> *only reveal the anger that is already in us.*
> Mary and Sam Peeples, *Parenting: An Heir-Raising Experience*

You both need lots of personal space, and your relationship will possibly not include much cuddling, kissing, or hugging. But you can still form a special bond with your Boxwood by listening without criticism, accommodating intense emotions, and being appreciative rather than demanding.

BOXWOOD TREE PARENTS AND THEIR SAPLINGS

A Boxwood Tree parent and a Palm Tree sapling

You two see the world differently—you are serious about most things, and your Palm Tree is serious about almost nothing! You'll do best to change your slightly negative, critical tendency so as to approach your optimistic Palm Tree with warmth. Ask yourself, "Does it really matter?" before reacting sharply.

Your Palm Trees don't have the same standards and attention to detail as you do, so express clearly what you expect or their first attempt may be well below the mark.

You might not want to stand out, but your Palm Tree wants to be different. Enjoy the unique nature of your Palm Tree, and be mindful that attempts to change your child to fit into a Boxwood mold will feel like rejection.

You may easily notice the things your child doesn't do perfectly and overlook all the charming aspects of your Palm Tree's exceptional nature. You may see things in black and white and believe yours is the only right way. Allow for your Palm Tree's inventiveness.

Learn to play and relax with your Palm Tree, even if you don't have much inner child in you. It's a gift of free therapy!

Your need for a large personal space can easily cause you to pull back when your Palm Tree wants to hug or kiss or constantly be close to you. Just remember how important these intimate gestures are for your Palm Tree, and bite your lip if need be. If you can learn to enjoy it, all the better!

Consider how quickly children grow up, and never wish away your Palm Tree's childhood just because you want to see maturity and responsibility in your child. And remember that your Palm Tree keeps you young at heart.

Your Palm Tree will play on your feelings to save her every time she has been irresponsible. Don't give in! Let her learn from the consequences of her own mistakes.

> *The greatest gift you can give your children are the roots*
> *of responsibility and the wings of independence.*
> Denis Waitley, *Raising Confident Kids*

A Boxwood Tree parent and a Rose Bush sapling

Boxwood Tree parents usually admire their Rose Bushes' sense of responsibility, hardworking nature, and perseverance but don't appreciate their stubbornness. Keep the rules simple but clear, and establish the rules with your child's input so you agree from the outset on what is expected.

You probably tend to micromanage things. This will drive your Rose Bushes up the wall because although they want to know the end result you expect from them, they also want to do things their own way. Keep your distance and don't ask questions with the purpose of advancing your own agenda.

Rose Bushes know that you tend to take things personally and sense when you feel guilty. They may verbally attack you, accuse you of being unfair, and drain you emotionally. Distance yourself emotionally from the hurtful behavior, and handle it calmly and rationally. It may help to say to yourself, "I did the right thing; I don't need to feel bad. Their emotions are not my responsibility to fix."

Although you see every single mistake, not every one of them is worth pointing out. Fight the battles that are matters of principle, such as those about character and morality. Leave the matters of preference alone—such as how they fold the laundry or organize homework.

A Boxwood Tree parent and a Pine Tree sapling

> *Anything we do for our kids that they can*
> *do for themselves, cripples them.*
>
> Michelle Shelton, "Did You Get the Hidden Parenting Message in *Finding Nemo*?"

Because Pine Trees can be unhurried and unmotivated, you feel like you give a string of never-ending instructions (usually loaded with threats) morning, noon, and night. You probably include incentives, time limits, and way too much detail. This could make your Pine Tree helpless and dependent. Say one clear thing at a time.

As a Boxwood parent, you are prone to having high expectations and standards; be mindful that this could make your laid-back Pine Tree feel like a failure. Who he is should be more important than what he achieves, shouldn't it?

> *Parents, don't come down too hard on your*
> *children or you'll crush their spirits.*
>
> Colossians 3:21

Try to reduce the pressure and criticism in your words, and replace them with appreciation for each attempt your Pine Tree makes—whether successful or not. Use your gift of observation to notice the positives.

Refrain from revisiting past mistakes. Pine Trees want to fix things but can't travel back in time to do that for you. Few things make them feel more helpless than a postmortem of their failures.

You have the ability to listen compassionately and understand an introvert's complex emotions. Use this insight to make your Pine Tree feel loved.

Neither of you are comfortable with verbal arguments. Conflict paralyzes a Pine Tree. If you have an argument, get over your hurt as soon as you can and say clearly, "It's over, and I'm not unhappy anymore. Are you also ready to forgive and move on?"

PINE TREE PARENTS AND THEIR SAPLINGS

A Pine Tree parent and a Palm Tree sapling

Palm Trees usually find their Pine Tree parents too placid—even boring. If you have a Palm Tree, you may need to plan creative, surprising, fun times with them; otherwise, your relationship with your Palm Tree could lack the sparkle it can have.

Palm Trees sometimes use Pine Tree parents' kindheartedness and avoidance of conflict against them. Look out for this, and prove yourself to your Palm Tree by monitoring important disciplinary targets. Insist on obedience.

Your Palm Tree probably knows that you don't like spoiling the fun and will approach you rather than the stricter parent. Consult your spouse before granting your child's wishes!

Don't let your Palm Tree manipulate you with melodrama. If you give in just to stop the tears, she'll put up an even bigger show next time, knowing that her moods can move you.

Pine Tree parents sometimes ask me where a Palm Tree's "off" button is located. It is understandable that their on-the-go nature can become too much at times. Try to enjoy your child's uniqueness and playfulness. Beware of enforcing your definition of maturity (self-control and emotional restraint) on this tree type.

Pine Tree parents typically don't want their children to experience any pain, so they often feel compelled to defend them, help them, and be constantly at their side, thus keeping them as content and safe as possible. Be careful not to overprotect your Palm Tree. He needs adventure, daring games, and space.

Palm Tree children will need your full attention for at least a few minutes every single day, not just a habitual question about their well-being every now and then. Your need for alone time could get you stuck behind a book or in front of the computer, smartphone, or television screen when your child needs you.

Palm Trees need a lot of physical contact. Get close to this child and give a lot of hugs and kisses. Play rough contact games with Palm Tree boys and pamper Palm Tree girls whenever you have energy to spare.

A Pine Tree parent and a Rose Bush sapling

> *God's servant must not be argumentative, but a gentle listener and*
> *a teacher who keeps cool, working firmly but patiently with those*
> *who refuse to obey. You never know how or when God might sober*
> *them up with a change of heart and a turning to the truth.*
> 2 Timothy 2:24–25

Because they want to keep the peace at all costs, Pine Trees are a manipulative Rose Bush's favorite target. If you try to avoid all conflict with your Rose Bush, you will get nowhere with your parenting.

Your initial response may be to withdraw from this angry, intense, noisy child. But that could jeopardize your chance at a great relationship. Stay close to your child despite the occasional thorn prick. The roses they will yield are worth it.

Rose Bushes only respect parents who can act with conviction and guts. You will sometimes have to act much more firmly than you feel comfortable with. If you have shown once that you are serious, you only have to give "the look" later on.

> *Parents who are too weak, too tired, or too busy to win make a*
> *costly mistake that will haunt them during their child's adolescence.*
> *If you can't make a five-year-old pick up his toys, it is unlikely you*
> *will exercise much control during his most defiant time of life.*
> Dr. James Dobson, *The New Dare to Discipline*

Because acting out is not your style, you may find it challenging to deal with your Rose Bush's outrage. Read the section on this in chapter 5, and practice applying it. Because you have a peacemaking temperament, you probably won't enter the conflict emotionally. Remind yourself that you are the parent, with God's mandate to set these difficult little ones straight.

Rose Bushes always have goals and reasons for what they are doing. If you want them to do something they did not initiate, be prepared to explain your aim and reasoning.

Be proactive when disciplining your child, especially in the teenage years. Think ahead about the challenges awaiting you, and try to be one step ahead of this challenging child. That will make up for the times when he catches you off balance.

A Pine Tree parent and a Boxwood sapling

Your even-tempered nature predicts that your Boxwood's emotional—and sometimes irrational—behavior may be your biggest challenge. If you negate her emotions because you can't handle them, she could experience rejection and have trouble entrusting her heart to you. Your warmth, listening skills, and gentle touch will make up for this.

Work on your communication with your Boxwood child if you find your conversations challenging. Read the section on this in chapter 6 for tips.

Because you see the core of the matter, you can teach your Boxwood how to keep things in perspective when he feels overwhelmed. A Pine Tree's shade brings sanity to everyone, especially Boxwoods!

To you, who your child is, is likely more important than what your child does. However, even though achievements are not important to you, please value them for your Boxwood child's sake.

Boxwoods are serious about fairness and justice, rules and regulations, while you may be comfortable with a few exceptions for the sake of peace. Make an effort to be fair and consistent in your actions so your Boxwood can trust you.

Because Boxwoods can be somewhat demanding, you will often want to switch off just to keep from burning out! Do not withdraw from your child, because you can be the best parent for her if you apply your patience, your forgiving nature, your sensitivity, and your knowledge of people.

TREES FROM THE SAME PLANTATION

When a Palm Tree raises a Palm Tree
Both of you are dreamers, which means you will be the ideal parent to inspire your child to reach his highest goal. Use your optimism to fan your child's ideals. Every child needs someone to say, "Yes, I believe you can!"

> *Always listen to experts. They will tell you what*
> *can't be done and why. Then do it.*
> Robert A. Heinlein, *Time Enough for Love*

Your temperaments are the recipe for a constant battle for attention. Palm Tree parents and their children can easily get jealous of one another because of this. Take care that you, as the adult, don't act childishly by begrudging your child the spotlight. Your aspirations to be young and cute forever can threaten your Palm Tree teenager, especially if you hack your way into your child's circle of friends.

You are both fun loving and not very concerned about duties, schedules, time, and details. You will have to distinguish between your roles as educator and playmate. As the parent, you need to set the example of self-control for your child. He will not learn this naturally.

Your own experiences can help your child avoid typical Palm Tree traps. Talk honestly and humorously about your mistakes and what you have learned from them. Being a Palm Tree, you most likely have a few stories worth telling!

If your spouse is a stricter tree type, you may be tempted to leave the discipline to him or her. Be careful not to put your friendship with your child ahead of your role as a parent.

> *Friendship is the relational goal of parenting, not the starting point.*
> Gary Ezzo, *Growing Kids God's Way*

When a Rose Bush raises a Rose Bush

Be specific about each one's areas of control; otherwise, you will have territorial fights morning, noon, and night. At a parenting talk, a Pine Tree mom asked what to do with all the conflict between her Rose Bush husband and son. A fellow Pine Tree mom with experience of this dilemma quipped, "Just keep out of it and mop up the blood. It's never fatal."

Remember that your Rose Bush grows up quickly; your attempts to control her life could make her very rebellious. Let her do everything that she is able to handle responsibly. She will make you proud if you expect no less than her best!

Your competitive spirits mean that you will enjoy contests, but remember that you are the adult and she is just a child. Don't crush your child by always being the winner. You are stronger than your child, but the way in which you show this is important. Maintain your self-control, love, and patience as best you can, because it is natural for you to break through the defenses of your opponent.

You expect submission from your children, so your Rose Bush's behavior will easily seem rebellious or defiant. Avoid being too rigid. Answer questions with good counterarguments, and make clear which things are negotiable and which things aren't.

Keep your instructions as short and sweet as possible and avoid reasoning. Your child will respect you if you can stay self-assured and collected.

You're likely in one or more leadership positions where you can set your little future leader a great example of godly leadership.

When a Boxwood raises a Boxwood

> *Lord, make me quick to admit when I'm wrong*
> *and easier to live with when I'm right.*
> Author unknown

You and your child will probably bring out the unyielding black-and-white characteristics in each other. Most of your clashes will be about trivialities that you both feel strongly about—things like which shoes would go best with an outfit or which part of the work should be done first. Learn to step back and get perspective when no spiritual principles, issues of integrity, or moral values are at stake.

You can anticipate many things that could possibly go wrong. When you express these fears, your naturally anxious child may add them to his already large collection of concerns. Teach him how you deal with fears and worries constructively, so he can do the same.

You probably want to know every little detail of your child's life, but your Boxwood wants privacy. Learn to respect this. Because you value your relationship, never search your teenage Boxwood's room, read his text messages, or go through his belongings, unless you have reason to believe your child is in trouble. Admit that you did it, and explain why. If you find something worrisome, make sure you are calm before addressing the issue.

Because both of you are likely emotional and slow to move on when you have been hurt, you will get much practice in the art of peacemaking. Be the first to try to patch up the relationship after conflict, and the first to forgive.

You and your Boxwood will probably be tempted to play on each other's guilty consciences. Boxwoods may manipulate you into taking the blame for their wrong choices. Don't be too quick to believe that their mistakes are because of yours, and beware of ascribing your moods to their misbehavior. Kids are never responsible for a parent's psychological well-being.

Your emotional insight will make you your Boxwood's potential best friend someday. You'll share deep thoughts and feelings with understanding.

When a Pine Tree raises a Pine Tree

Your Pine Tree child will most readily follow your example. Try to set an example worthy of imitation.

Because you both may have difficulty talking about your feelings, it can be difficult for you to build a deep relationship. Invest time in your communication, and use other means, perhaps hugs and silent side-by-side time, to build a bond.

Maybe your child has only a few interests, just like you do. Because you understand the cruelty of excessive pressure, you are the ideal person to patiently help her discover her passion, provided you have embraced your own passion in life.

You may believe everything is fine as long as there is peace. However, don't always trust the silence. Observe your child carefully.

You probably resist the rat race and busyness of the school calendar. Still, try to make the effort to attend sports tournaments and other events where your child will need your encouragement.

Be careful not to indulge your child's passive nature too much. You can make your inactive child even more flaccid by having low expectations and setting an example of passivity.

Because you tend to make things comfortable and easy for your children, you can potentially stand between them and the consequences of their actions. Children sometimes have to fall and get hurt on the road to adulthood. Set aside your nurturing nature when your child is ready for little lessons about "real life."

Discipline is not what we do in order that our children will love us; it is what we do because we love our children.
Ronald Morrish, *Secrets of Discipline for Parents and Teachers*

CHAPTER 9

HYBRID TREES

In this chapter:

- What to do when your child is a combination of two or more tree types.
- Young Palm-Roses
- Young Box-Palms
- Young Pine-Palms
- Young Pine-Roses
- Young Box-Roses
- Young Box-Pines

Parenting is tough enough without all the natural clashes, isn't it? Add the inevitable temperament differences, and life gets really intense. Perhaps you can identify with these families who have found hope and humor in the clashing personalities God put together:

Ewald is an eight-year-old Box-Palm. His mom is a Boxwood Tree. When they both wake up a little grumpy, and Mom has been up since 5:00 a.m. to get the family set for school and work, life gets a little sour. Fortunately, Dad has a Palm Tree side to his personality and knows how to wake up little Ewald in a way that gets him up on the Palm Tree side of the bed: Some mornings he storms into the room, yelling, "The Philistines are upon you!" Or he pretends to look for Ewald's head on the other end of the bed, asking why he is all turned around. Sometimes he uses funny ringtones or songs on the cell phone to bring out Ewald's Palm Tree side, and the morning is saved!

Sometimes children can be three tree types rolled into one, like three-year-old Katie. She is a Contra-Rose (the term we use for those who are everything but Rose Bush). Katie has the peaceful Pine, the performer Palm, and the perfectionist Boxwood inside her. One day she got upset when her parents wouldn't let her drink from the dog's water bowl. She threw her own version of a tantrum by standing right next to her mom with her face against the wall, silent, but with tears streaming down her face. Katie doesn't do throw-down tantrums, but when she's upset, she makes sure there's someone around to witness her sulking.

A Saturday morning can get interesting when Mom and Dad have opposite ideas of fun, as one family recently told me: The Contra-Pine dad (Rose Bush, Palm Tree, and Boxwood combined) planned an early morning mountain-bike outing for the family. His idea of fun was to wake at 5:00 a.m. to be on the mountain by six. Naturally, he didn't think it was funny when his three-year-old Palm Tree, Emil, came shuffle-dancing down the hall wearing all the pairs of underwear he could get his hands on, covering his legs from the floor up to his bottom! This was *his* idea of Saturday fun—cheering up the household with his antics. All Dad saw was a delay in his plans.

Pine-Rose Mom's idea of weekend fun is sleeping in and waking up to coffee and a fresh newspaper, so her underwear-shuffle-dancing son didn't amuse her either. It only meant that the floor would be decorated with an assortment of undies for her to pick up later. Pine-Rose teen Mikael woke up to spot his underwear among Emil's collection and realized that Emil had crossed the holy boundary into his room. Cue the questions: "What is *wrong* with you?! What part of *boundary* don't you understand?" Mikael demanded that his underwear be sterilized before he would ever wear it again!

All this commotion woke up Pine Tree Etienne, a preschooler with autism. He wondered what on earth was going on with his people, then concluded that Mikael, who doesn't like hugs, definitely needed a long hug. (Mikael's reaction to this is unfit for publication in a Christian parenting book.) Youngest brother Peter, a highly excitable Box-Palm, was fortunately still asleep. As Emil's faithful apprentice, he undoubtedly would have cracked up at the sight of his older brother wearing all that underwear and probably would have found some more underpants and joined the shuffle-dance party.

Contra-Pine Dad was quick to see his 6:00 a.m. adventure flying out the window, realizing that "family bonding" was probably not the best idea at that moment. Pine-Rose Mom exclaimed that if only everyone had decided to sleep in, none of this would have happened!

WHAT TO DO WHEN YOUR CHILD IS A COMBINATION OF TWO OR MORE TREE TYPES

In more than 60 percent of adults and children, temperament is a combination of two tree types. Often the types are related—for example, both are task oriented or both are energetic and driven—but sometimes there is extreme diversity within one person. And on occasion this can be confusing.

If, for instance, one-half of my son's temperament is outgoing (Palm Tree) and the other half is a bit shy (Pine Tree), whether he is spirited or shy will depend on his unique combination and the situation. He will possibly appear to be more of a Palm Tree in familiar surroundings, such as at home with his family, and more of a Pine Tree at school. If, however, he is the youngest child and dominated a bit by his brothers, he may seem more like a Pine Tree at home and perhaps express his Palm Tree traits at school.

When your children's temperaments are a combination of tree types, familiarize yourself with all the types and deal with each characteristic separately, instead of searching for a different label. If you have a sapling who doesn't look like any of the combinations outlined below, it simply means that you have a sapling with more diverse features.

Between 7 and 10 percent of children and adults have a combination of three tree types in their temperament mixture. The information from the previous chapters also applies to them. For instance, if you have a Contra-Boxwood child (everything but Boxwood Tree), you may deal with your child's aggressive outbursts according to the Rose Bush chapter, have serious conversations with her according to the Pine Tree chapter, and find the discipline techniques for Palm Trees most effective.

Because combinations and ratios between the dominant temperament types can vary so much, your child might not be exactly like the description, but you may see many similarities. Your child's individualized Tall Trees Kids Profile Report will give a much more thorough and accurate description.

Young Palm-Roses

Many parents agree that Palm-Roses are the naughtiest of the types by far because of their combined urge to discover and conquer. Unnecessary rules and control only worsen their behavior! Unless they have a creative teacher, these guys will have trouble doing "boring" schoolwork. They need active education if they are to excel academically.

I will try to put this as gently as possible: Palm-Roses are not very teachable when it comes to social graces. Their parents may find that it takes their Palm-Rose four or five years to master the manners their other children learned in just one year.

Manners are as slow to develop as self-control. But Palm-Roses usually develop physically more quickly than other tree types because they are constantly seeking new challenges. They are regularly testing and improving their own abilities. As a result, they often excel in demanding, aggressive, and contact sports.

They enjoy control and attention equally. They can reason effectively from an early age and will alternate charm and anger to get what they want.

Palm-Roses usually want to do everything and participate in all that life offers. Of course, they also want to be the best at everything! Unfortunately, they don't have the same follow-through as the Box-Roses, making many of their pursuits flashes in the pan.

Palm-Roses can be loud and impulsive, may lack self-control, and more than any other children can embarrass their parents by blurting out personal remarks. While I was pregnant with my third child, a young dad recognized me on a beach and approached me with a remark about my first parenting book and how it helped him discipline his Palm-Rose four-year-old, who promptly disproved it by pointing and exclaiming, "Look at her fat, fat belly!" Palm-Roses can completely take charge of social situations because they are charming leaders. But they need help finding the right balance between bossiness and teamwork.

Many bullies are Palm-Roses who are ruled with an iron fist at home, then want to take back control somewhere else. Or they get so little attention that they yearn for any reaction, however negative it may be.

Palm-Rose teenagers can be the rudest of all unless they have been trained to respect other people's feelings.

In addition, young Palm-Roses:

- are the most prominent chatterboxes and therefore some of the cutest children—full of jokes and original sayings, and quite outgoing
- have the best self-image of all the combinations and like to sing their own praises
- have the worst temper tantrums of all and take a long time to learn to control their emotions
- have the most energy and vitality and are easily misdiagnosed with hyperactivity and other attention deficit disorders. If we don't focus on the positive side of this and realize that they are on

their way to becoming productive, active, inno-
vative adults, we can clamp down on them too
hard and extinguish their flame.

Young Box-Palms

Box-Palms are more of an emotional challenge than a disciplinary one because they are a combination of two emotional tree types.
They require a lot more attention and encouragement than Pines and
Rose Bushes and need to be handled with great empathy and patience.
Because they want to please other people so much, they can simply be
compliant in return for love. We need to ensure that they understand
not only what we expect but also why it is the right behavior.

Their intense need for acceptance makes them overly sensitive
at times, and the slightest angry look or harsh word can upset them.

Because Box-Palms are often melodramatic and fond of words,
they make excellent actors, storytellers, motivational speakers, writers, and poets.

Usually when parents complain that they can't identify their
child's type and can say only that she is "confusing," the child has this
combination. Owing to the contradictions in this combination, the
child can behave so differently from day to day that the parents can
never predict how the child will act. Box-Palms can moan, rejoice,
giggle, nag, and pull a long face in surprisingly quick succession.
However, if we can remember to treat them like Palm Trees when
they are happy but like Boxwoods when they are sad, it will be less
confusing, and we'll help them regulate how they feel.

In addition, young Box-Palms:

- often have imaginary friends and extensive fantasies
- have a huge capacity for spiritual things; thanks to their childlike faith, they easily build relationships with the Lord from an early age
- can be drama queens and moaners par excellence
- need help to find a balance between time alone and social time, work and play, so they don't get overtired
- are popular because they are talkative, fun loving, and caring toward friends
- are the moodiest teenagers, are susceptible to peer pressure, and are most likely to experiment, especially with their appearance
- will try to manipulate you emotionally, a tendency that you must nip in the bud firmly

Young Pine-Palms

Pine-Palms have the potential to be the most forgetful, absentminded, and careless of all—absolute dreamers on another planet. They have the least inner drive, but because of this they are also often the most compliant. They care what other people think of them and like to keep their parents happy. Pine-Palms can be easy to rear (only needing "the look" sometimes), except for the challenge of instilling a sense of responsibility in them.

They usually want to rest or play, one of the two. The tongue-in-cheek saying "Who wants to stand if you can sit, and who wants to sit if you can lie down" probably originated from their neck of the woods. Work is not likely their first priority!

Pine-Palms can have short attention spans and are often labeled with attention deficit disorder. (They are not usually as prone to being hyperactive as Rose-Palms may be.)

The Pine-Palm's greatest need is for peace and happiness. They experience harsh discipline as disapproval and rejection, and because they have such trouble dealing with conflict, verbal or physical violence at home can devastate them.

A Box-Rose mother (performance driven) burst into tears at one of my seminars when she discovered both her children were fun-loving Pine-Palms. "They won't get anywhere in life!" she cried out, upset. When I told my husband this, his answer (also being a Pine-Palm) was: "Tell her we don't care how far Box-Roses get in life, and we hope they never come back, because they're party poopers!"

Pine-Palms also:

- usually do well in the social sphere at school but may suffer academically and become underachievers
- struggle with time management, and tend to put off starting a task, so their work is rarely finished on time
- don't typically have aspirations of leadership, but they are usually chosen first for teams because they are excellent team players
- are usually happy, easy babies—friendly and adaptable
- have the least task orientation and self-discipline of the six combinations; therefore, they take a long time to become reliable

- usually are animal lovers and like people of all ages, as is evident from this conversation between six-year-old Pine-Palm Joshua and his mom:

> Mom: How was school today?
>
> Joshua: It was good.
>
> Mom: Who did you play with?
>
> Joshua: I played with Jacques and Stefan and Hanno and Louwrens and Viljoen and Jordaan and Ruben … and everyone.
>
> Mom: What about Alissa? Did you play with her?
>
> Joshua: I played with her the day before yesterday, and I will play with her again another day.

Young Pine-Roses

These little kids often appear to be more mature than average because they are the most rational (and also the least emotionally challenging) of all the combination types.

Pine-Roses are, however, probably the most stubborn of all the temperament types because they have the Rose Bush urge to be in control and the Pine Tree tendency to be obstinate. They usually create an impression of independence because they want to do their own thing on their own, and they reject supervision or help.

The Pine Tree typically cancels out the explosive nature of the Rose Bush to such an extent that Pine-Roses have good control over their emotions, which may make them seem aloof and hard to read.

In addition, young Pine-Roses:

- are usually not very social or exuberant; they have only one or two good friends
- can divide their attention between the goal and their friends
- are often chosen as leaders even if they are not invited to all the parties
- often excel in schoolwork and individual sports; this is possible when their determination combines with their interest in a specific field
- tend to be abrupt, and it takes time to build a warm, deep relationship with them
- don't often seek physical contact with their parents, so meaningful connection has to be made on other levels

Young Box-Roses

Box-Roses are often achievers because of their determination and their ability to think of details and the ultimate goal.

They are also often critical and may demand the best from everyone—as they do from themselves. Unfortunately, this means they can be blind to their own mistakes when it suits them.

Box-Roses can be plagued by fears and worries, which usually stem from those things they can't control. Four-year-old Pierre has the same serious prayer request every night: "Mommy, please pray that I won't have to watch bad stories in my eyes tonight!"

Their hugs and kisses may be scarce, and the parents can easily feel as if their children don't like them. But touch is simply not their main language of love. They thrive on compliments, appreciative words, and increasing responsibilities as they grow older. They will experience this as love too.

Box-Roses have a strong will from day one. At only three months, Box-Rose Leilani demonstrated her strong will by crying every time her aunt asked her if she would go to sleep. She cooperated as long as the word "sleep" was not involved in her bedtime routine. Any other conversation was welcomed with sweet baby sounds.

Box-Roses are determined to do what they learned is the best course of action, as feisty little Nika, age four, demonstrated. Nika's parents taught her to scream and kick and punch around if someone ever grabbed her and held her tightly. However, they failed to mention that the appropriate list of recipients for such violence did not include her grandpa! When she was visiting her grandparents for a week, all by herself like the independent young lady she is, she got so upset about something that her grandpa picked her up and held her tightly to help her settle down. Nika's programming kicked in, and she gave her grandpa a sudden whack that nearly knocked him off his feet. She continued to kick and hit, while yelling to boot. Isn't that what Mommy said to do?

Box-Roses also:

- drive themselves to fulfill their responsibilities without much encouragement
- are reliable, task oriented, and model students, unless they have a serious conflict with a Rose Bush teacher

- are extremely independent and self-reliant (unless the Boxwood component is dominant, in which case they may cling to their mothers in their baby and toddler years)
- tend to stay in a bad mood for a long time
- are serious and usually don't respond well to jesting or silliness in others
- become angry when embarrassed
- are the keepers of order and enforcers of rules— regular little generals
- have an inconsistent self-image; when they perform well, they are proud and self-confident, but a small failure can give their confidence a knock
- are tenacious; they have the perfectionism of a Boxwood combined with the perseverance of a Rose Bush

Young Box-Pines

These double introverts can be the dreamiest combination because of their low energy levels and extremely calm nature. The less one expects of them, the more relieved they are. Box-Pine Timmy, four years old, had a fever. When his mom told him he was very hot, his remark was quite positive. "Yay! I don't have to go to school."

They can be musical or artistic (usually when the right brain is dominant), but they don't like performing onstage. When they are left-brain dominant, they are technical or scientific in their thinking. A classic example is a Box-Pine friend of mine (who happens to have both the scientific and the musical gifts of this combination) who took his eight-year-old Box-Pine son (a trains, planes, and automobiles type of Box-Pine who'd rather watch machines move) to the theater, fully aware that it would not be a highlight. The boy never complained but slept through the concert. When his mom asked if he enjoyed it, the diplomacy that is so typical of this combination tree type came out faultlessly. "With all the beautiful lullabies that man sang, I just couldn't stay awake!"

Box-Pine saplings also:

- often seem to be the easiest babies: good sleepers, well adapted to routine but not dependent on it
- usually are exemplary and compliant because they crave approval and fear conflict
- are slow to complete tasks, get dressed, eat, and tell a story because all the details or methods must be completed exactly right
- seem shy and timid, slow to adapt to preschool, and not keen on kissing even relatives
- need advance notice of change, which they do not like
- need preparation when the family is going to move or when a new sibling is on the way
- can be full of whims and fancies but are not rebellious or moody
- are prone to acting selfish and will protect their possessions with a vengeance
- appear to be the victim but often incite other children to carry out the mischief they contrived

LET'S GET PRACTICAL

Determine how well you understand grafted trees by choosing the right answer to each of these questions. The answers appear at the end.

1. Which grafted tree type is Oprah? Think about her success as a businesswoman and her unbeatable talent as an interviewer. She inspires and influences millions of people worldwide to believe in their dreams and realize them. She doesn't cling to the past—she focuses on contemporary matters.

    a. Box-Pine
    b. Palm-Rose
    c. Pine-Palm
    d. Box-Rose

2. Which grafted tree type was Esau? He was a hunter and a nature lover. Think of his impulsive exchange of his birthright for some lentil stew. When Jacob stole his blessing on top of this, he was angry, but he didn't want to commit murder while his father was still alive. He didn't even attempt to follow Jacob. Later, he was so happy to see his brother again that he embraced him in tears, gave him gifts, and immediately forgave him.

    a. Box-Pine
    b. Palm-Rose
    c. Pine-Palm
    d. Box-Rose

3. Which combination of three tree types was Joseph? He divulged all his dreams, was apparently comfortable in his stand-out clothing, and stayed optimistic throughout his hardships. He was trusted with many responsibilities by all his superiors because of his work ethic. He had exceptional leadership and strategic abilities. He was very emotional when he was reunited with his brothers, but he was also very strict with them. He manipulated them but eventually forgave them all their wrongdoings.

a. Contra-Pine (Boxwood, Rose Bush, and Palm Tree combined)

b. Contra-Palm (Boxwood, Rose Bush, and Pine Tree combined)

c. Contra-Boxwood (Rose Bush, Pine Tree, and Palm Tree combined)

d. Contra-Rose (Boxwood, Pine Tree, and Palm Tree combined)

4. Which grafted tree type is Bill Gates? He is one of the richest people in the world, thanks to his success with Microsoft, but he doesn't have a very prominent public image. He has repeatedly defended the monopoly of his company successfully, and he is a philanthropist who without any fanfare appropriated millions of dollars for fighting AIDS and tuberculosis in Africa, among other ventures. He is rational and known for his excellent conflict-resolution skills.

a. Box-Pine

b. Palm-Rose

    c. Pine-Palm

    d. Pine-Rose

5. Which sapling is grafted into a Palm Tree if the grafted tree is a disciplined athlete who practices come rain or shine?

    a. Rose Bush

    b. Boxwood Tree

    c. Pine Tree

6. Which grafted tree type will likely be most devastated by their parents' divorce?

    a. Pine-Rose

    b. Box-Rose

    c. Palm-Rose

    d. Box-Pine

Answers: 1b, 2c, 3a, 4d, 5a, 6d.

CHAPTER 10

KEEPING PERSPECTIVE

When we start applying guidelines from a book like this one, questions and uncertainties will confront us. We may tie ourselves up in knots overanalyzing the profiles, and we can easily lose perspective when one small thing between us and our children doesn't seem to improve. The guidelines below are meant to help us keep perspective. You are welcome to read them from time to time when hailstorms threaten to destroy your harvest.

Remember that your relationship with the Lord forms the basis for all your relationships, especially your relationship with your children. The Father-child relationship between the Lord and you will be the foundation and the frame of reference for your parenting. This relationship has to be healthy.

Seize the opportunity to lead your children to the Lord at a tender age. When the Holy Spirit shapes your child's heart from the inside while you direct it from the outside, parenting becomes a wonderful adventure. Our influence alone is not enough. We need the Lord's influence on our children's spirits as well!

Give your children what they need to thrive before you expect them to give back what you require. Reread what your saplings need in order to thrive before you punish more severely, present greater rewards, or grab at new techniques. A child who receives his tailor-made "fertilizer," those things necessary to make him feel that he has dignity and is loved, likely will not be unruly.

Never lose sight of the fact that your children have wills of their own. Your task is to lead your children, not drag them. Sometimes they will tug at every restraint; sometimes they might even break loose. The natural road to maturity requires that they want to follow their own minds. The older they get, the more choices they need to control. You will be held accountable only for things you have control over, and should have control over at each stage. Whether a five-year-old brushes her hair before she goes to school will be up to you. At that stage it will be your responsibility. However, when she is eighteen, it will be unacceptable if you still insist on brushing her hair. This well-timed surrender of control is difficult, especially when it affects delicate matters such as teenage relationships and entertainment choices. In these decisions our children want to take over the reins. But we should never forget about the protective potential of prayer! Prayer for God's intervention can be much more effective than our intrusive restraints.

Follow through with the practical plans and intentions you have made as a result of reading this book. Knowledge hasn't changed anybody's life; only actions have! Parenting is not a warm and fuzzy feeling you get when you take your child onto your lap. Parenting is a thousand little sacrifices of time, attention, and love, which we ought to make unconditionally. We understand that our children are only lent to us by a God who will hold us accountable for them. Praise the Lord for His willingness to equip us with knowledge!

Avoid measuring progress in terms of small matters such as table manners, tidiness, or school report cards. Instead, ask the important questions: Am I helping my children build a growing relationship with the Lord? Do my children and I have a bond characterized by comfortable communication, even when we argue? Do my children have the abilities and principles to build lasting and healthy relationships with other people? Am I busy helping my children develop a unique character?

Make sure your children are physically healthy and nurtured to the extent that it is in your hands. Children who eat well, sleep enough, are physically active, have time "to be children" and play, and get help in areas where they are challenged do better with discipline. Allergies, stress, too much refined food, and a lot of "screen time" cause them to become moody and more difficult to teach and discipline.

You don't need to struggle along on your own. Parenting well means parenting in community. Get help, unashamedly seek advice, and attend parenting talks or seminars, even when you think you've heard it all.

Bury your idealistic pictures of perfect children (or parents) so that you can enjoy your children just as they are. Disciple them prayerfully as they mature into the identity God designed for them. Occasionally, sit back and observe the beauty of their personalities. Celebrate how they have already grown in their God-given nature. They will change you and the world for the better!

SPANKING AND THE BIBLICAL MANDATE

Parents often fear that any punishment, and especially spanking, may be traumatic. I once heard someone explain it this way: If you walk into the kitchen, put your hand on a red-hot stove plate, and burn it, you won't be traumatized, just burned. If, however, the stove comes to your room in the middle of the night and blisters you in your bed, then you'll be traumatized!

Punishment is not equal to trauma. Predictable consequences are the key. Unpredictability causes trauma. Someone once told me that, as a child, he prayed each morning that his mother would be a witch that day. It would be less traumatic than wondering every day who he would have to deal with—his mother the witch, or his mother the angel. This child was spanked less often than I was, but his "spankings" came in the form of unexpected slaps across the face. Usually he had no idea what he had done wrong. That is trauma. The spankings I received as a child, however, were predictable. I knew what was coming because I was punished for willful disobedience. That was never traumatic and always well deserved.

Read Proverbs 20:30.

> *Blows and wounds scrub away evil, and*
> *beatings purge the inmost being. (NIV)*

> *Blows that wound cleanse away evil; beatings*
> *make clean the innermost parts. (NRSV)*

> *Stripes that wound scour away evil, and strokes*
> *reach the innermost parts. (NASB)*

> *A good thrashing purges evil; punishment goes deep within us.*

Consider the following questions:

- Do you think this scripture refers to the spanking of a child?
- What, according to this scripture, are grounds for corporal punishment?
- Indicate, according to this biblical mandate, the behaviors from this list that would warrant "blows" to cleanse away "evil": willful defiance, forgetfulness, back-talking, carelessness (such as losing possessions), intentionally dangerous behavior that threatens the child's or others' safety, challenging an authority figure, hyperactivity and attention deficit disorder, lies intended to deceive

or get others into trouble, childishness, impulsiveness, wetting the bed, accidents (such as knocking over a glass at the table), emotional meltdowns, behavior caused by shyness (such as not greeting people politely), violence against others, manipulation, a slow work pace.

Would you agree that less than half of the misbehaviors mentioned above fall in the categories of "evil" and "willful defiance"? Only when a person knows exactly what is expected, has the skills and maturity to act appropriately, and still makes a decision to do the wrong thing, fully knowing that it is wrong, will I confidently say that the person has acted with evil intent. Every other behavior may be better met with training, empathy, professional help, and patient guidance.

Parents who have never spanked their children, and are proud of how their children have turned out, may have raised kids who never displayed dangerous, illegal, or intentionally defiant behavior, or the parents don't view rebellion as a serious matter in their own or in their children's lives. The parents may put a high premium on assertiveness and confidence and may have felt that defiance was simply the evidence of these traits in the making.

Read Proverbs 23:13–14 and 29:15–17 and Hebrews 12:7–11.

Don't be afraid to correct your young ones; a spanking won't kill them. A good spanking, in fact, might save them from something worse than death.

Do not withhold correction from a child, for if you beat
him with a rod, he will not die. You shall beat him
with a rod, and deliver his soul from hell. (NKJV)

The rod and reproof give wisdom, but a child who gets his own
way brings shame to his mother.... Correct your son, and he
will give you comfort; he will also delight your soul. (NASB)

Wise discipline imparts wisdom; spoiled adolescents embarrass
their parents.... Discipline your children; you'll be glad
you did—they'll turn out delightful to live with.

A rod and a reprimand impart wisdom, but a child left undisciplined
disgraces its mother.... Discipline your children, and they will
give you peace; they will bring you the delights you desire. (NIV)

Endure hardship as discipline; God is treating you as his children.
For what children are not disciplined by their father? If you are
not disciplined—and everyone undergoes discipline—then you are
not legitimate, not true sons and daughters at all. Moreover, we
have all had human fathers who disciplined us and we respected
them for it. How much more should we submit to the Father of
spirits and live! They disciplined us for a little while as they thought
best; but God disciplines us for our good, in order that we may
share in his holiness. No discipline seems pleasant at the time, but
painful. Later on, however, it produces a harvest of righteousness
and peace for those who have been trained by it. (NIV)

For the time being no discipline brings joy, but seems sad and painful;
yet to those who have been trained by it, afterwards it yields the
peaceful fruit of righteousness [right standing with God and a lifestyle
and attitude that seeks conformity to God's will and purpose]. (AMP)

After you have considered these and other scriptures, discuss the following statements with your spouse or another parent. Make up your mind about your beliefs, so you will be consistent in your actions.

Pro-spanking views:

- A spanking can change a bad attitude, not just unacceptable behavior, thus making a child less rebellious and more trainable.
- An effective spanking must be painful but not humiliating because it is not supposed to be an emotional message, but rather a physical one.
- In the Bible, the word *discipline* is strongly related to painful consequences.
- The Bible presents spanking as an acceptable way of correcting.
- The Bible recommends spanking especially for young children.
- If we never give our children a spanking for rebellion, this could make us an accessory if they go astray.

- If we spank and also lovingly train our children, depending on the type of misbehavior, they learn the difference between punishment for crimes and correction for mistakes, which are both parts of everyday life.
- Parental discipline is proof of parental responsibility. Some children may read our lack of painful discipline as a lack of commitment to parenting them.
- A spanking eventually leads to pleasant outcomes, even if it is unpleasant for parent and child in the thick of things.

Uncertain and anti-spanking views:

- The Bible leaves room for discipline without spanking.
- We should spank only gently and with care.
- A biblical spanking can easily break a child.
- The fact that warning, training, and punishment are mentioned here means that I have to talk and train, with spanking as an absolute last resort.
- If I don't feel like spanking, I don't have to do it, because if it *feels* wrong, it *is* wrong.
- We should use our hand so that we don't unintentionally go too far.

- Spanking is violence and will breed only violence in a child. The New Testament discourages violence.

Should spanking be illegal?

Many who oppose corporal punishment accuse Solomon (and God) of cruelty and want to proverbially throw out the "corporal punishment" baby with the Old Testament bathwater. However, Proverbs is a book of wisdom, full to the brim with lessons in self-control, gentle words, compassion for others, and confirmation that anger is foolishness. It is in this context that spanking appears. It should go without saying that the Bible doesn't give us the right to do any of the following: grab a rod without thinking, spank other people's children, punish a child in anger, hit until you feel better, spank in retaliation, punish a child for behavior that was not intentional, give a spanking without explaining to the child what you are doing and why, spank in a humiliating way by pulling down a child's pants for example, or punch with fists, give a child a shove against the chest, or slap a child in the face.

These scriptures address parents' fear of a correct spanking. They also reassure parents that painful discipline within the context of a healthy parent-child relationship doesn't harm a child; in fact, spanking could protect our children from far worse consequences. Why do you think the aspect of protection is pertinently emphasized? I believe it's for the reasons listed below. Discuss these statements with another parent until you are sure of your own convictions:

- The Lord knows that good parents don't want to hit their children and that they need the assurance that the short-term unpleasantry will yield long-term fruit.
- If you always want to be loving toward your children, it is difficult to spank them. Calling painful discipline a proof of fatherly love and commitment brings it into perspective.
- Many parents want to protect their child's body more than their child's undying spirit and need to be reassured that physical pain can have spiritual benefits.
- Even in biblical times some parents thought spanking would break a child's spirit. These and other scriptures help them and us understand that while abuse could do that, there are nonabusive ways to spank.
- The Lord warns against neglect of painful punishment because He may hold us accountable if we don't discipline firmly.

There are many differences between parents who abuse their children and parents who advocate a biblical spanking.

Abusive parents are usually uninvolved, indulgent, emotionally detached from their children, and uninterested in good parenting practices. They don't like being included in the daily needs and nurturing of their children, and when their children frustrate them, they are likely to overreact.

Research has found that child abusers seldom touch their children lovingly; there is little contact except for the abuse. These parents often lack insight and resources. Because of circumstances, a lack of support, and their own childhood wounds, they may see their children as an emotional, physical, financial, and practical burden that can be alleviated through abuse (for example, shaken if they cry too much). They may see children as property that they can treat as they wish ("I brought you into this world, and I will take you out of it if you don't do what I say!"). Physical violence doesn't occur in isolation but is part of a pattern of abuse that may include verbal aggression, neglect, and sexual abuse perpetuated by these parents from experiences they grew up with.

Parents who intentionally follow a biblical approach to parenting, on the other hand, are usually involved parents who know the importance of emotional bonds with their children. They see their children as treasured gifts or loans for which God will hold them accountable. Their church community expects them to take their parenting task seriously. Those among them who spank their kids for disobedience believe that in doing so they are acting obediently toward God and trust that the promises of the Lord regarding the fruit of parental discipline will hold true. They make mistakes and may occasionally spank for misbehavior that doesn't warrant punishment, but they are typically taught and guided by the church community in this respect. Additionally, they usually have access to courses, biblical resources, and parenting advice, making ignorance over abuse less likely to occur.

The studies I have read concerning the harm done by spanking didn't look at the three most important factors simultaneously: the quality of the parent-child relationship, the type of behavior that was punished, and the exact manner in which the parent spanked the child. It should go without saying that even a mild spanking in anger from a disconnected parent for an accidental misstep would be harmful. That outcome cannot be generalized to predict harm to a child spanked calmly by an affectionate parent for playing with his dad's laptop after being told that he would be spanked if he did. Children's experience of punishment correlates with their experience of their relationship with their parents. A child who feels safe in a loving home will eventually perceive even a severe spanking with a leather belt as having had no psychological ill effect, while an abused child may experience even a rude word as a shattering humiliation.

Years ago I had an unfortunate incident at my aftercare center. The children were playing with rocks left over from renovations. Without thinking, I threatened to spank the child who dared to throw another stone. As I turned to walk to my office for a meeting, a defiant fourth grader, whom I will call Terrance, picked up a stone and hurled it at my car. Forty-five pairs of ears had heard my threat, and now forty-five pairs of eyes were on Terrance and me. I took him to my office, where I obviously did not keep anything to spank kids with. This was a place for kids at risk and the last thing they should experience is any form of violence.

I explained to Terrance that I wasn't angry (though I may have felt otherwise had the rock not missed my car!). I said, "Terrance, I want you to know that you can always count on me. If I say I will help you, I will. If I say I will spank you, I will do that too. I am going to keep my promise because you knew what would happen and threw the rock anyway." I constructed a creative plan and held true to my promise. I made the spanking count, knowing it would probably be the only one he ever got, because he clearly had never had one and said as much too.

Then I waited for his father, who was described to me as a "Napoleon," to arrive with the police in tow. Nothing happened for weeks. Then, one morning, his mom called me. "I don't know what happened between you and Terrance. He won't tell me, but this morning I decided that I've now had enough of my husband's abuse. I told Terrance we needed someone to help us get to a place of safety. He told me to call you. He said if you promise to help us, you will keep your promise."

If that spanking was abuse, why would Terrance think I could help him and his mom flee domestic violence? Laws that equate everyone's experiences fail to acknowledge these distinctions that even a fourth grader can understand. If we want spanking to be made illegal because some parents spank excessively or for the wrong reasons, we should also make hugging and kissing our children illegal because of the actions of pedophiles. A law against spanking in a family context will not prevent bad parenting; it will only prevent good parents from acting wisely. Parents who have self-control and who have the best interests of their children at heart are not the problem. Education for those who act abusively and who misunderstand childhood behavior would go much further to solving the problem.

Examine your spanking habits.

For what behaviors do you give a spanking, even if your child would not be spanked for them according to biblical principles?

For what behaviors do you *not* give a spanking, even if the Bible recommends a spanking for your child?

Why do you feel your punishment works better for these behaviors than a spanking would?

Do you spank with calmness and control, or do you "lose it"? How might you stay calm when you discipline your child?

Which of the following messages will be conveyed by a controlled, calm spanking (C) and which ones by an angry spanking (A)? Indicate them and contemplate how you could change your way of spanking.

Your behavior is unacceptable. C/A
I am very angry now. C/A
I don't like you. C/A
I will feel better after hitting you. C/A

I will feel the same whether I spank you or not, because it is not about me. C/A

I spank out of conviction. C/A

I spank to teach you something. C/A

I spank to hurt you. C/A

I still love you. C/A

I love you when you behave and hate you when you misbehave. C/A

I punish you because I have to, even when I don't feel like it. C/A

I don't like punishing you. C/A

Think about the behaviors for which you unnecessarily give spankings, then write down an alternative for each of them. Remember that punishment is the answer to a small subset of misbehaviors, many of which your child may never display. Some children simply don't defy (usually Pine Trees or Boxwoods who avoid conflict and mistakes, and Palms who are eager to please). Most undesirable behavior simply means the child needs better instruction.

Keep in mind that we as parents model God's heart to our children. His training in our lives only rarely involves a painful intervention. It is mostly guidance through the voice of His Word and His Spirit—a kind Voice at that—that leads us back to the best path (Romans 2:4).

NOTES

1. Gary Smalley, *The Key to Your Child's Heart* (Dallas: Word, 1984).

2. Strong's Concordance, s.v. "*dar·kōw*," Bible Hub, accessed September 16, 2017, http://biblehub.com/hebrew/darko_1870.htm.

3. Barnes' Notes, "Proverbs 22," Bible Hub, accessed September 16, 2017, http://biblehub.com/commentaries/barnes/proverbs/22.htm.

4. Strong's Concordance, s.v. "*derek*," Bible Hub, accessed September 16, 2017, http://biblehub.com/hebrew/1870.htm.

5. Charles F. Boyd, *Different Children, Different Needs: The Art of Adjustable Parenting* (Sisters, OR: Multnomah, 1994).

6. Some characteristics in this section are adapted from the descriptions of personality types by Cynthia Ulrich Tobias, *You Can't Make Me, but I Can Be Persuaded: Strategies for Bringing Out the Best in Your Strong-Willed Child* (Colorado Springs: WaterBrook, 1999); and Florence Littauer, *Personality Plus for Parents: Understanding What Makes Your Child Tick* (Grand Rapids, MI: Fleming H. Revell, 2000).

7. Ross Campbell, "How to Show Love through Physical Contact," chapter 5 in *How to Really Love Your Child*, 3rd ed. (Colorado Springs: David C Cook, 2015).

8. From an article by Francesca di Meglio, "Four Signs Your Kids Are Lying," formerly available at www.lhj.com.

9. Tobias, *You Can't Make Me*, 50–51.

10. James Dobson, *The New Dare to Discipline* (Carol Stream, IL: Tyndale House, 1992), 96.

11. Mark Brandenburg, "Dads, Don't Fix Your Kids," newsletter, May 2005.

12. Smalley, *Key to Your Child's Heart*, 29.

13. Caroline Stanley, "How Kids Decide If You Are Fair," American Academy of Pediatrics (2005).